A Restless Spirit

· THE STORY OF ·

ROBERT FROST

by Natalie S. Bober

Henry Holt and Company · New York

First published in 1981 by Atheneum
Revised and expanded edition published in 1991 by Henry Holt and Company
Published by Henry Holt and Company, Inc.,
115 West 18th Street, New York, New York 10011.
Published simultaneously in Canada by Fitzhenry & Whiteside Ltd.,
91 Granton Drive, Richmond Hill, Ontario L4B 2N5.

Library of Congress Cataloging-in-Publication Data
Bober, Natalie.
A restless spirit : the story of Robert Frost / Natalie S. Bober.
New rev and expanded ed.
Includes bibliographical references and index.
Summary: A biography of the famous American poet, detailing the
events of his frequently unhappy life, his love for his wife and
children, and the way all of this was woven into his poetry.
ISBN 0-8050-1672-4
1. Frost, Robert, 1874–1963—Juvenile literature. 2. Poets,
American—20th century—Biography—Juvenile literature. [1. Frost,
Robert, 1874–1963. 2. Poets, American.] I. Title.
PS3511.R94Z555 1991   811.52—dc20   [B]   91-13970

Printed in Mexico

3 5 7 9 10 8 6 4 2

The following have generously given permission to use excerpts from copyrighted works:
From *The Poetry of Robert Frost*, edited by Edward Connery Lathem. Copyright 1916, 1923, 1928, 1930,
1934, 1938, 1939, 1947, © 1967, 1969 by Holt, Rinehart and Winston. Copyright 1936, 1942, 1944,
1951, © 1956, 1958, 1962 by Robert Frost. Copyright © 1964, 1967, 1970, 1975 by Leslie Frost Ballantine,
© 1966 by the estate of Robert Frost. *Robert Frost: The Trial by Existence*, by Elizabeth Shepley Sergeant.
Copyright © 1960 by Elizabeth Shepley Sergeant, © 1988 by Ann T. Gugler.
Reprinted by permission of Henry Holt and Company, Inc.

Contents

Robert Frost

Acknowledgments

Many people have played a part in this book, and to all of them I owe a debt of gratitude. At the very beginning, Kathleen Morrison encouraged me to write about Robert Frost, and spoke enthusiastically of the need for a biography of him for the young adult. I gained much insight into the poet from Alfred Edwards, who with his lovely wife, Eleanor, first talked to me of his friend as we lunched on their terrace with its breathtaking view of the Green Mountains, where he had walked with Robert Frost. Edward Connery Lathem, then dean of libraries at Dartmouth College, took time from his busy schedule to reminisce about his friend, and made the letters of Robert and Elinor Frost to Sidney Cox available to me at the Baker Library. Dr. Theodore Grieder, Fales Librarian, opened the Frost Collection at New York University to me, providing a wealth of resources.

Hal, Sandie, and Steven Samuels offered many thoughtful suggestions. Very special thanks to Steven, himself a kindred "restless spirit," for the suggestion of the title of the book.

To B. J. Dennis, whose special friendship has spanned many years and many miles, my gratitude for introducing me to Robin Hudnut.

In my recent research for this new edition many more people helped bring the poet alive for me. Claire Ternan opened the Derry farm and escorted us through with a running commentary on the Frost family's life there. Donald Sheehan, curator of the Frost farm at Franconia, drove there from Dartmouth College on a glorious fall day to share new insights on the poet with me in rooms filled with Frost's presence.

Philip Cronenwett, chief of special collections and curator of manuscripts at Dartmouth College, made the entire Frost collection of photographs available to me, as did Daniel Lombardo, curator of special collections at the Jones Library in Amherst. Mr. Lombardo also graciously made it possible for my husband to photograph many of the Frost treasures in the library's collection. Helyn Townsend at the Herbert H. Lamson Library at Plymouth State College also helped to make my picture search a joy. And Eartha Dengler, executive director of Immigrant City Archives, did considerable sleuthing to locate photographs and information on Lawrence, Massachusetts, at the end of the nineteenth century.

Robin Hudnut once again shared memories of her grandfather as well as a treasure trove of family photographs. For these, for her search for the perfect picture of San Francisco, for putting me in touch with Carla Schmitt Sanders, but mostly for the treasure of her friendship, my gratitude and my love.

I have been fortunate in having had two editors with whom I enjoyed working on this book: Marcia Marshall, who guided me through the first edition; and Adrienne Betz, whose vision made a new edition possible. Both have offered sage advice, faith, and friendship. To both I am deeply grateful.

My mother, Dolly Birnbaum, did not live to see this new edition. But it was she who early taught me the patience and perseverance necessary for careful, accurate, and thorough research, and who painstakingly proofread and corrected the original manuscript and indexed the book.

The greatest thanks of all are due my husband, who traveled with me through "Frost Country," took hundreds of beautiful photographs, and sorted through even more with me in libraries and colleges along the way. His patience, encouragement, love, and faith in me have truly "made all the difference."

Introduction

Robert Frost, the first poet ever to be invited to speak at the inauguration of a president, has been hailed as America's "national bard," its "poet laureate," and "the best-loved poet in the country." I would have liked to have known him. The poignant image of the white-haired poet who proudly stepped up to the podium at the inauguration of John F. Kennedy and then was unable to read the poem he had written for this occasion remains etched in my memory.

It was on that bright, snowy day in January of 1961 that I decided I would try to learn all I could about Robert Frost. I began to reread his poems. The more I read of the poetry, the more I wanted to read about the man who had written those poems, and the more I read about Frost, the more I wanted to share him with others.

Robert Frost called to me as a kindred restless spirit. This farmer, teacher, poet moved back and forth, not only across a continent but across the Atlantic Ocean as well in order to support his family and further his poetry. I came to admire not only the gentle old New England poet but also the enthusiastic young poet who had the courage to start on nothing more than a dream and faith in himself. "It was instinct that kept me going in the direction I took," he said.

Revered late in life as the "poet laureate of Vermont," Robert Frost actually spent the first eleven years of his life in San Francisco. A shy, lonely, sickly little boy, he was terrified of his father's sudden violent outbursts of rage, yet he adored him. He was afraid to go to school, and didn't read a book by himself until he was fourteen years old. In spite of this, by the age of seventeen he had become the class valedictorian and had fallen in love with the girl he would eventually marry. And he had found the courage to trust his own feelings, and to make what he called "the reckless choice."

"When I was young," he once said, "I was so interested in baseball that my family was afraid I'd waste my life and be a pitcher. Later, they were afraid I'd waste my life and be a poet." He smiled gently and added, "They were right."

He was the student whose restless spirit caused him to walk away from Dartmouth College, and later from Harvard. Yet he became a teacher who called himself a "book person," a "reckless reader," and told his students that anyone who bought a hundred dollars' worth of books would get an A. "All things and all stories go on in books," he said.

Robert Frost's poetry appears simple, but the writing of it must have been anything but simple. True poems, Frost believed, never begin in a deliberate fashion. Rather, they begin "as a lump in the throat, a sense of wrong, a homesickness, a lovesickness." "A poem begins in delight and ends in wisdom," he said. "For me the initial delight is in the surprise of remembering something I didn't know I knew."

And he always made use of metaphor, the comparison of two things that have one unexpected quality in common. "Every thought is a feat of association," he said. "Thus all thinking is metaphoric. Metaphor is an attempt to say one thing in terms of another." When he tells us that

> *Two roads diverged in a wood, and I—*
> *I took the one less traveled by,*

he is not really talking about a path in the woods. Rather, he is telling us that he refused to conform to an expected pattern in order to please his family. He chose to go his own way: he was a rebel who took the road less traveled, and that "made all the difference."

He was a natural talker who was drawn to other talkers—he loved to gossip—and he often said he liked people for their voice tones before he liked them for themselves. So it is probably not surprising that he would attempt to bring alive a conversational tone in his poetry. What is surprising is the extraordinary effort and determination he put forth to perfect this technique to the point where he forged a new and original world of poetic art.

One of his most significant contributions to the craft of writing was his theory about the sound a sentence makes. "We write of things we see and we write in accents we hear," he said. "All poetry is to me first a matter of sound. I hear my things spoken." Real poetry for him required the tones of natural speech, *and* it had to be metrical. The familiarity of meter and rhyme (the familiar beat) is comforting, he said, when we are attempting to read and understand something new. He liked to compare it to putting a straight edge on a curve. He gave to his verse a casual atmosphere, as though he had just met a friend and stopped to chat with him, but there was a careful artist behind this, one who made his rhyme and meter carry out his intention more exactly, and give the poem its subtle power. He told his students that poetry was a fresh look and a fresh listen. It's the combination and arrangement of the words—"the turn, the twist, the wiggle, at least."

It was the poetry that first drew me to Robert Frost, and continues its strong hold on me. And it was the poetry that inspired me to look more closely at the man who wrote it. All the qualities that I discovered about him in my research made me refuse to let go of him, even after the original publication of this book in 1981. Since then I have continued to read and reread his poetry, and have learned so many new things about him that I was delighted when the opportunity to share him with a new generation of young readers was presented to me.

I have tried to portray the human being behind the facade of the great poet, all the while showing how the poetry was an outgrowth of the life he lived. With this goal in mind, I have woven into the text of this new edition many more poems and photographs in the hope that as you read his story, you will be able to visualize Robert Frost in his surroundings, and will feel that you are there at the birth of the poems, experiencing, with him, the excitement of the poem being "made."

His aim was always to "make" the best poems he could, to have them published, and to ensure their survival in the world. This he accomplished full measure. And through it all, this restless spirit gently but firmly refused to conform.

A Peck of Gold

Dust always blowing about the town,
Except when sea fog laid it down,
And I was one of the children told
Some of the blowing dust was gold.

All the dust the wind blew high
Appeared like gold in the sunset sky,
But I was one of the children told
Some of the dust was really gold.

Such was life in the Golden Gate:
Gold dusted all we drank and ate,
And I was one of the children told,
"We all must eat our peck of gold."

Some of the dust was really gold

They were a study in contrasts as they walked along to-gether, the young boy almost running in his struggle to keep pace with the man's long, sure stride. The child, frail, fair-skinned, dreamy-eyed, his extraordinarily large blue eyes set deep under a high forehead, his blond hair blowing back as he hurried along, seemed very different from the man—so tall and handsome, with jet black hair, thick sideburns, a neatly trimmed mustache, and steely blue eyes, a revolver bulging in his pocket. It was hard to believe they were father and son.

It was June of the year 1884, and ten-year-old Robert Frost and his father were hurrying through the streets of San Francisco toward the newspaper office of the *Bulletin*. While other boys Rob's age were confined to a classroom, Rob was sharing the adventure of this so-phisticated city with his father, helping him track down a story for the *Bulletin*.

William P. Frost, Jr., Rob's father, was one of the many people who had flocked to California after gold had been discovered there in 1849. He, like others, had hoped to make his fortune there. Now he was working as a newspaper reporter, and entering politics as well.

At noon the pair stopped at Levy's Saloon on Bush Street, the gathering spot for newspapermen and politicians. It was Rob's favorite place. This summer, when the Democrats had nominated Grover

Cleveland for president of the United States, they nominated William P. Frost, Jr., for San Francisco city tax collector. At Levy's, while his father drank his beer and whiskey with the other men, Rob could help himself to the bountiful free lunch offered there.

But first, before he tasted any, Rob took one of his father's printed cards announcing that William P. Frost, Jr., was the Democratic candidate for tax collector, and put a thumbtack into it. Then, with a silver dollar held flat beneath the tack to act as a flying hammer, he hurled the small poster upward to stick into the board ceiling. Rob had become quite adept at attaching the cards to the ceiling in this manner—without having to climb—and was secretly proud of the way his father's friends regarded this newly developed skill. He liked knowing that it was he who had been responsible for prominently displaying his father's cards on the ceilings of all the saloons in downtown San Francisco. He considered himself very lucky, too, that his father allowed him to carry messages to city hall, to distribute handbills on street corners, and sometimes even to listen to his impromptu soapbox speeches made on the spur of the moment. He was grateful for anything that brought him closer to his father, this man whom he idolized at the same time that he feared him.

Rob had been born in San Francisco on March 26, 1874, nine

Robert Lee Frost, at age seven months. *Courtesy Dartmouth College Library.*

years after the conclusion of the Civil War. It was a difficult time, a time when two antagonists—North and South—were struggling to become one again. It was a time, too, when San Francisco was a lawless, roaring, exciting town, a city of courage and luck. Violence was still a part of San Francisco life, and many men carried guns. So the doctor who came to the house on Washington Street to assist his mother in the delivery of her child was probably not surprised at the threat his father made. William Frost warned the doctor that if anything happened to his wife while their baby was being born, the doctor would be shot. Fortunately, the revolver was not needed, and mother, child, and doctor all survived. The baby was named Robert Lee Frost, after the Confederate hero his father admired. His mother was not consulted on the choice but she—and later his wife—always called him Rob, his Scottish nickname.

Rob's mother and father were very different from one another. William P. Frost, Jr., brought up in Lawrence, Massachusetts, where his father was the foreman in a cotton mill, had been a wild and unmanageable child, constantly defying his strict and puritanical parents. As a youngster, William often roamed the streets looking for trouble. When his despairing parents tried to lock him in his room at night, he climbed out the window and down a homemade rope ladder. As a teenager he once ran away from home, hoping to enlist in the Confederate army of General Robert E. Lee, but was picked up by the police in Philadelphia and brought back home. When he entered Harvard College he gambled, drank, ran around with women, yet managed to graduate with honors and a Phi Beta Kappa key.

After graduation in 1872, William Frost's adventurous spirit was stirred by tales of the Far West, and he decided to go to San Francisco. He was an eager, restless young man, anxious to be on his own in a new land, to see this city that was considered then to be the wickedest in the world, and anxious also to be independent of his disapproving parents.

On his way west, when he ran out of funds, William stopped in the little town of Lewistown, Pennsylvania, and secured a job as principal of a small private school. It was there that he met and fell in love with Isabelle Moodie, the only teacher on the staff. Her beauty and intelligence captivated him, and he quickly persuaded her to marry

LEFT: William Prescott Frost, at the time of his graduation from Harvard College, 1872. *Courtesy Jones Library, Amherst.*

RIGHT: Isabelle Moodie Frost, three years after her marriage to William, 1876. *Courtesy Dartmouth College Library.*

him, despite the difference in their age and religion. Isabelle was six years older than William, and a devout Scotch Presbyterian. William was descended from the earliest Puritans to settle in New England.

Isabelle Moodie had been born in Scotland and had been brought to the United States when she was twelve years old. Tall and graceful, with beautiful dark brown eyes and thick auburn hair, her aristocratic bearing gave evidence of her social and cultural background. Her father had been a sea captain, but the uncle who had brought her up in Columbus, Ohio, had been educated at the University of Edinburgh and was a prominent and prosperous banker. The hint of a burr in Isabelle's lively, musical voice, reminiscent of her Scottish heritage, made her all the more appealing to William.

Isabelle Moodie and William Frost, Jr., were married on March 18, 1873, just six months after they had first met. Isabelle was twenty-nine years old, William only twenty-three.

They remained in Lewistown until the completion of the school term. In June they set out for Columbus, Ohio, where Isabelle had grown up, for a visit with the bride's family and friends. William remained for a short time. Then, seeing his wife happily settled with her family, he left for San Francisco alone, promising to send for her just as soon as he could establish himself as a newspaper reporter and find a home for them.

William Frost traveled by train on the newly completed Union Pacific Railroad, arriving in Oakland, California, on July 9, 1873. As he boarded the ferry for the short trip across San Francisco Bay, the sea gulls wheeled after the ferryboat in endless changing patterns. In front of him San Francisco appeared to be a mountain island rising abruptly from the sea, and the sails of the three-masted schooners entering and leaving the harbor seemed to take on a golden hue whenever the sun hit them. He felt certain that he had made the right decision. He knew that he would be successful here—would become a well-known and highly regarded journalist. All he needed to complete his happiness, he thought, was Isabelle at his side.

He quickly landed a job as an editorial writer and reporter for the *Evening Bulletin*, one of San Francisco's leading newspapers. By November he had an apartment, and was ready to send for his wife. She bravely made the long journey across the country alone. She was already pregnant, their child due to be born in four months.

The San Francisco that Robert Frost was born into that following March consisted of block after block of narrow, two-story houses, bay windows protruding from many of them in order to catch a maximum of sunshine and light. In this city of frequent fog and chill winds, bay windows in the front parlor and in the master bedroom were more a necessity than a luxury. The streets were paved with cobblestones or planking, and board sidewalks ran alongside them.

There were many steep hills in San Francisco, and as Rob grew up he loved to climb these hills with his mother. Together they would walk to the top of Telegraph Hill or Russian Hill or Nob Hill, the three highest in the northeast section. From them Isabelle could point out to Rob that San Francisco was almost an island, with the Pacific Ocean on the west, San Francisco Bay on the east, and the Golden Gate Straits on the north. From Telegraph Hill also, he could see the many sailing schooners going to faraway places. He saw also the tall clipper ships bringing goods from the East Coast of the United States and from the Orient. Steam schooners brought lumber for local building, and took other cargo north to Puget Sound and Alaska.

They watched ferryboats like the one his father had come on as they made their twenty-minute run from ferry slip to ferry slip. The sails of the schooners often seemed to Rob, as they had to his father years before, to be made of gold. The strait linking the bay with the ocean was referred to as the Golden Gate, because of the way it shone in the sunset. There was even talk of someday building a bridge across the Golden Gate.

As Rob and his mother walked about the city, they noticed that even the dust that was always blowing had an aura of gold about it. Rob thought some of it must really be gold and wrote later:

> *All the dust the wind blew high*
> *Appeared like gold in the sunset sky,*
> *But I was one of the children told*
> *Some of the dust was really gold.*

Isabelle also took Rob on trips around the city by horse trolley, or by the newer cable car. Public transportation had been expanding during the 1870s, and by the time Rob was born, several companies were operating horse-drawn streetcars between the business center of the city and the outlying industrial and residential areas. Andrew Hallidie's plan to bury a moving cable in a slot beneath the trolley tracks, to which the cars could be attached by a device called a "gripping clamp," had also been put into operation, and in October 1873 the first of the city's cable cars began to jerk up Clay Street. Rob loved to ride the cable cars, their constant clanking sounding to him like a muffled freight train.

Sometimes Rob and his mother became so absorbed by the sights and sounds of San Francisco that they found themselves still out as dusk began to settle over the city. It was these times that Rob loved best, for then he could watch as the lamplighter came round with his torch and ladder. He would stare in wonder as the lamplighter placed his ladder against the lampposts, then climbed up and ignited the gas jets so that the flames glowed softly up and down the streets.

These were happy times for Rob, times he would remember and cherish as he grew older. But life in San Francisco was not always happy for him.

As Rob was growing up he was at first unaware of the tensions that were beginning to pull his mother and father apart and that, ultimately, were to take their toll on him as well. Years before, when Rob was tiny, Isabelle was so occupied with him that she perhaps failed to notice that her husband was beginning to drink and gamble. She had never before seen this side of him. In this city where there were more bars than restaurants, and where most people had come on the big gamble of finding gold, it was easy for William to revert to his old college habits. His adventurous temperament thrived on the atmosphere of this raw city built on chance.

Often he would come home at night drunk. Whiskey seemed to transform him from a solicitous and protective husband into a brutal man. Often Isabelle was forced to run into the street with Rob, or to a neighbor's house for fear that her husband's drunken violence might kill them.

Left alone much of the time, and unaccustomed to the ways of a frontier town, Belle, as most people called her, gradually began to find consolation in prayer and in church work. Her neighbor, John Doughty, was then minister of the Swedenborg Church, called the Society of the New Jerusalem, and Isabelle decided to join.

Emanuel Swedenborg had established this society when he found that he had the power of second sight and could converse with spirits and angels. The society seemed to offer Isabelle the mysticism that her imaginative, story-loving nature needed, but William would never attend services with her.

She found a friend in one of her husband's associates, though, and came to rely on him for advice and guidance. He was Henry George, the crusading editor of the *Evening Post,* at the height of his career as a fearless journalist interested in politics and intent on exposing public abuses. He had somewhat of a steadying influence on William, and in 1875 hired him away from the *Bulletin* to work for him. This association was to last for nine years.

Despite William's apparent reversal, under Henry George's influence, to his old, calmer days, Isabelle was not convinced. When she found that she was expecting another child, she confided to Mrs. George she was so fearful of the harm her husband's violence might do that she was planning to leave him. The same competence Isabelle

Rob often saw this view of the schooners in San Francisco Bay when he walked with his mother in 1883. *Photograph by Carlton E. Watkins, courtesy California Historical Society, San Francisco.*

found necessary to survive in a frontier town also made it possible for her to uproot her child and abandon her husband. It was indicative of her strength of character that she was able to explain to William exactly what she planned to do. She secured enough money from him for travel expenses and, with the then two-year-old Robbie, journeyed across the country by train to the home of her husband's parents. It was there, in Lawrence, on June 25, 1876, that Rob's sister Jeanie was born.

But both Rob and his mother were unhappy in Lawrence. None of the warmth and affection they had hoped for was forthcoming. In fact, his grandparents, stern, straitlaced puritans, seemed to blame Belle for their son's bad habits, and so, as soon as possible after Jeanie was born, the three left Lawrence.

They were welcomed into the home of a close friend of Belle's, Sarah Newton, in Greenfield, Massachusetts, and remained there throughout the summer despite William Frost's many apologetic letters to Belle, begging her to return. The congenial family atmosphere here, with its overtones of deep religious faith, was exactly what Belle needed. But it had taken its toll on her little boy. Uprooted from his home, taken away from his father to live with unloving grandparents in a strange environment, and then having to cope with a new baby sister who usurped much of his mother's time and love, Rob became a very confused and unhappy little boy.

At the end of the summer Belle finally decided to return to San Francisco and her husband. When they arrived, at the end of November 1876, after the seemingly endless trip by coach across the prairies, Belle found a husband apparently overjoyed to see her, his two-and-a-half-year-old son, and the baby daughter he didn't know.

But she found also that while she had been gone her husband had accepted the challenge of a famous walker, Dan O'Leary, and had competed with him in a six-day-and-night walking race, popular at that time. Tickets were sold to spectators, some people placed bets on one or the other of the opponents, and witnesses and judges were hired to determine the winner. The men walked for a designated period of time, being free to sleep as much or as little as they felt necessary. William Frost had often competed in this sport—and won—during his days as a student at Harvard. He boasted that he had won this race also, but O'Leary refused to pay his bet. He claimed that Frost had violated the rule that the walker's forward heel must always touch the ground before the other foot was lifted from the ground. Far greater than the frustration of losing the bet was the tragic result. The strain of the physical exertion had brought on consumption (today known as tuberculosis).

At this point Belle resolved to do the best she could and threw herself into the role of wife and mother. She seemed to accept her husband's weaknesses and tried to deal with them. She was determined to make her marriage work.

It was not an easy task. William quickly reverted to his old habit, using the excuse that the whiskey he so loved was "medicine" for his illness. He still displayed quick flashes of anger and cruelty. These often came unexpectedly, immediately after a display of affection and love. Also, there was an almost constant lack of sufficient money. There were many moves back and forth from an apartment to a hotel, partly because Belle's background had not trained her to cope with household chores. (They had twelve addresses during their eleven-year stay in San Francisco.) All this made for a difficult relationship between husband and wife and an unsettling atmosphere for a shy and sensitive little boy.

Once by the Pacific

The shattered water made a misty din.
Great waves looked over others coming in,
And thought of doing something to the shore
That water never did to land before.
The clouds were low and hairy in the skies,
Like locks blown forward in the gleam of eyes.
You could not tell, and yet it looked as if
The shore was lucky in being backed by cliff,
The cliff in being backed by continent;
It looked as if a night of dark intent
Was coming, and not only a night, an age.
Someone had better be prepared for rage.
There would be more than ocean-water broken
Before God's last *Put out the Light* was spoken.

· 2 ·

There would be more than ocean-water broken

When the time finally came for Rob to go to school, he had developed so many fears that he viewed the prospect of leaving his mother with terror. On the first day of school the long bus ride to the private kindergarten only added to his agony. When another little boy pushed him too high in a swing during recess, he became sick to his stomach and his fear was heightened. Later, on the trip home, the bus driver had difficulty finding Rob's house, and Rob became alarmed that he might never see his mother again. Belle met him at the bus stop and he ran weeping into her arms, protesting that he would never go to school again.

And he never really did go to school in San Francisco. The next day, when he complained of stomach pains, his mother allowed him to stay home. This became the pattern for the rest of his school "career." He seemed to develop severe stomach pains every time he was supposed to go to school, and his mother decided to teach him herself at home.

Belle was a capable teacher, but Robbie hated learning, and he progressed slowly. Belle was undaunted, almost smothering her son with the love and attention she couldn't give to her husband. When she couldn't interest Rob in learning to read, she read to him. She told him stories from the Bible, she told him the story of Joan of Arc who heard the voice of God speaking to her, and she told him of

Emanuel Swedenborg, the Swedish scientist who wrote of his communication with angels.

Belle also loved to tell Rob and Jeanie fairy stories, and these particularly appealed to Rob's imagination. Perhaps they even helped him to excuse his own blending of fact and fiction when he related a story. One of the children's favorites was *At the Back of the North Wind,* by George MacDonald, the story of a little boy whose real adventures were so closely interwoven with three fairy tales that he was unable to distinguish between his real world and his dream world.

Belle read poetry to Rob also. His most vivid memories, later, of her reading were of the romantic poetry that she loved. She read poems of Robert Burns, Edgar Allan Poe, and Robert Browning.

One day, when Rob was six years old and his sister Jeanie four, they realized that something important was about to happen. Their father had been elected a member of the California delegation of Democrats, and was being sent to Cincinnati, Ohio, to help nominate General Winfield Scott Hancock as the presidential candidate at the National Democratic Convention. While the children were probably too young to understand what all this meant, they were caught up in the excitement of the preparations. They were elated at being allowed to go with their father to the train—taking the cable car to the Ferry Building, then boarding the ferry for the trip across the bay past all the boats—the three-masted schooners, the fishing boats, the pleasure boats, the men-of-war—to the train shed in Oakland. There they reveled in the bustle of the brass band send-off and the cheering crowds. As the train pulled out of the station Rob must have blinked back tears as he waved good-bye to his father, and watched him standing on the rear platform of the last train, so handsome as he waved in return and doffed his new top hat to his well-wishers.

Rob had already built up a strong love and admiration for his father and he tried hard to emulate him. He loved just to be with him—to share his exciting man's world. He enjoyed the camaraderie of his father's friends—of their rough-and-tumble world, their extravagance, the fun he had with them. He was thrilled when they allowed him to tag along.

Rob and his sister Jeanie, ca. 1879. *Courtesy Dartmouth College Library.*

Later that summer Rob, who always slept with his door partly open because of his fear of the dark, was able to overhear many conversations that intensified the awe and admiration of his father's world. Committeemen and political friends often came to visit, and their talk of Civil War leaders and battles was exciting. Often he would lie awake, quietly listening to the talk, thinking that his father was even more the hero than Grant, Sherman, and Lee, and wonder if he, too, would someday be a hero.

But that same summer Rob's illusions about his father were shattered. His grandfather, William's father, had retired from his job and he and his wife were on their way west to see the country and visit their son. Excitement ran high in the Frost household on Grace Terrace. Rob was particularly pleased that their coming meant an opportunity for him to go with his father on the ferry trip across the bay to meet the train. The trip itself was always exciting, but for Rob to be able to spend all that time with his father was even more of a delight. He was in no way disappointed when, on reaching Oakland, they learned that the train had been delayed by snow avalanches in the Sierras. All that meant to the little six-year-old was the bonus of another ferry ride with his father.

When Grandmother and Grandfather Frost did arrive, Robbie did not recognize them. He had been too little when he had been in their home four years before to remember them.

The next morning Rob's open door made it possible for him to hear something very different from the exciting political discussions he was used to. He heard a bitter argument between his mother and father. He could tell by the clatter of the dishes and the silver that his mother was setting the table for a special breakfast for his grandparents. What Rob heard, though, surprised and upset him. As his father began to eat breakfast alone, not waiting for his parents to join him, Isabelle pleaded with him to wait just this one time and spend a few minutes with them. William, who had never gotten along with his father and was not happy at having his parents in his home, refused, then said he had to leave for work. William always hated the puritanical New England he had grown up in, and his father's coming was for him another reminder of his heritage. To William, his father represented New England, and he didn't want this reminder of where he had come from. Rob soon heard his mother call his father "a spoiled child." He heard his father threaten angrily, and then he heard the slam of the door as his father did, indeed, leave without breakfast, like a sullen little boy. Rob was confused and disappointed. He quickly forgot about this incident, though. Soon after his grandparents left to return to Massachusetts, his father allowed him to join in the excitement of campaigning for fall elections. For the little boy this meant parades with brass bands and floats to ride on, speeches to listen to, and errands to run to other politicians in the neighborhood. Once Rob even got to march with his father in a torchlight procession, and sparks from the torches fell in his hair. A new and greater closeness was building between father and son.

But it was a strange closeness. At the same time that Rob was becoming his father's companion, he was also learning to fear him. William Frost believed in the old adage "spare the rod and spoil the child," and often showed his anger at something Rob had done by whipping him with any handy weapon.

One day, embroidering a story to make it sound better, as he often did, Rob complained to his father that the grocer had called him a "son of a bitch." William, in a characteristic display of quick temper, grabbed the child by the arm, dragged him down the street to Mr. MacPartland's grocery store, and said to Rob, "Now tell me again what Mr. MacPartland called you."

Rob knew he was in a tight spot. If he stuck to his story his father might kill the grocer with one well-aimed blow from the cane he was carrying. If he told the truth his father's wrath would surely fall on him. He hesitated a moment, then said softly, "He called me a son of a gun." Then he stood still, head hanging, tense and waiting. As the blows from the cane began, he looked up to see the grin on Mr. MacPartland's face.

Another time, one Halloween eve, William refused to allow Rob and Jeanie to cut out pumpkins. He didn't want the mess that was certain to result from scooping them out. Rob and Jeanie didn't complain. They simply went to a friend's house and watched the other children shape the grinning faces. Later that evening, Rob's best friend arrived with a surprise present for him—a jack-o'-lantern all cut out, a burning candle inside to light the face.

Rob, upset by his father's ruling, and embarrassed by this display of friendship, blurted out that he was not allowed to have a pumpkin, and slammed the door. His father, seeing this, and probably embarrassed also by the exposure of his own selfishness, reached for the nearest weapon, which happened to be a metal dog chain. He lashed Rob's legs until they bled.

Isabelle fled to her room with Jeanie and prayed for mercy. She often tried to teach her children to seek consolation in prayer. She would read Bible stories to them about heroes who had overcome hardships through courage, skill, and wit, and through a persistent striving for honor and distinction.

On occasion, her method seemed to work. There was the day that Rob was sent by his father down to the corner for a bucket of beer. On the way home Rob, tossing the change in the air, dropped a dime. Horrified, he watched it bounce on the board sidewalk, roll downhill, then disappear through a crack. He tried in vain to retrieve it with a stick. When he could not, he thought of several stories he might tell to explain the loss. Then past experiences warned him he had best tell the truth, and he went home. He tiptoed into the house in the hopes that his father wouldn't hear him, and told his mother what had happened.

Belle, as fearful of William's wrath as Robbie, took the child into her bedroom, knelt with him, and prayed. Then she sent him to explain the incident to his father. Terrified, Rob stood before the man and blurted out in one quick sentence how he had lost the dime. The man looked at the boy absently for a moment, then said, "Never mind," and returned to the editorial he had been writing. Rob was certain that prayer had wonderful powers.

During the summer of 1883, when Rob was nine years old, his father and some of his journalist friends arranged an outing as a change from the dust of a San Francisco summer. The group of families pitched tents on the beach across San Francisco Bay near the beautiful village of Sausalito in Marin County. The fathers who were not on vacation could take the ferry from Sausalito to San Francisco every morning and return to the little tent colony each evening.

Soon after they arrived there, though, Belle realized that she had made a mistake in coming. The men played cards, drank whiskey, and practiced target shooting, using the empty whiskey bottles thrown into the bay as targets. This was not her idea of fun, nor did she particularly want Rob and Jeanie to witness it. But her objections were ignored.

One evening while they were there, William decided that long-distance swimming might help cure his consumption. He invited Rob to walk with him along the beach toward the Golden Gate. Then, leaving Rob alone on shore to guard his jacket, towel, and whiskey bottle, he recklessly swam through the icy water to an off-shore bell buoy. As the choppy waves began to hide his father from view, Rob became panicky. Watching anxiously for what seemed an interminable amount of time, Rob finally saw his father climbing the metal ladder on the buoy. He watched him stand there just long enough to regain his breath, then saw him dive off the swaying buoy into the water for the long swim back to shore. Again, fear began to build up in Rob as he watched in an agony of suspense as his father desperately fought the waves. Finally, William dragged himself to shore, totally drained. Relieved, but proud of his father's accomplishment, Rob ran down to the edge of the water, handed his father a towel, and watched him gulp down his whiskey.

Rob experienced a different fear of the water on another occasion. His father, celebrating a streak of luck in gambling, took his family to dinner at the Cliff House, one of their favorite restaurants. Rob and Jeanie particularly loved its view of the Pacific Ocean. After dinner they all walked down the long flight of wooden steps to the beach for a stroll along the shore at dusk. Robbie, absorbed in his own game of hitting stones with a whip he had made of seaweed, unintentionally dropped behind the others. When he finally realized that he was alone under the cliff, he became frightened. The roar of the waves, the towering wall of rock, the dark clouds reaching down, all seemed threatening. Terrified, he ran until he found his parents. Many years later his memory of this experience was translated into the poem called "Once by the Pacific."

At about the time Rob turned ten, he began to envy boys in a group called the Washington Street Gang. Before this he had not been old enough—or brave enough—to want to join them. Finally, he mustered enough courage to ask the leader, Seth Balsa, if he could join.

Seth responded by asking Rob if he could fight. Rob, secretly cringing at the thought of fighting, said, "Yes."

"Can you lick that kid over there?" Seth asked, pointing to Percy MacPartland, the grocer's son, who was not quite as big as Rob.

"I could lick two boys the size of Percy," Rob boasted, trying hard to conceal his fright.

Balsa obliged. He designated another boy about Percy's size, explained the challenge to the two boys, and the fight was on. Rob did his best, desperately trying to use techniques of fighting he had been watching for years. But while using one hand to attack Percy, he had to use his other to ward off blows from the other boy.

The fight lasted long enough to give the crowd of onlookers what they wanted most to see—blood coming from all three participants. Soon they were on the ground, punching, kicking, scratching. By the time Seth stepped in to separate them, Robbie's nose was bleeding, both his cheeks were bloody, and his lower lip was badly split. But the Washington Street Gang had seen enough. They were impressed with Rob's courage and ability, and they immediately made him a member. The warrior, hurt and on the verge of tears, went home to get his face patched up. Suddenly, as he was walking home, Rob realized what had happened—his courage had conquered his cowardice. He had grown up. He was as brave as his father.

But now Rob learned something else as well. He learned what it meant to belong to the Washington Street Gang. He learned to steal. When Seth needed a new pair of wheels for the wagon he used to coast perilously down the steep hills of San Francisco, Rob and Seth went to a house on Leavenworth Street known to have them, crawled in under the porch, and, after Seth had quietly jimmied the window, Rob had to squeeze in through the narrow opening. He quickly located the wheels, and handed them out. Impressed with the ease with which he had accomplished his mission, Rob looked for more. He also passed out a croquet set, but Seth drew the line at the Christmas tree ornaments Rob offered. When Seth's wagon appeared a few days later with shiny new wheels, Rob felt a sense of pride at his part in the crime.

On another occasion, when Rob and his newfound friends were returning home from an unsuccessful jaunt to the country to raid an apricot orchard, they passed the slaughterhouse where pigs were about to be killed. Rob remarked that he knew this slaughterhouse well. His father often took him with him when he went there to drink the fresh-killed animals' blood, a habit that nauseated Rob, but that William Frost thought would cure his consumption. At this disclosure, Rob was ordered to climb the fence and steal a pig. This he did willingly, climbing the fence and nimbly jumping down. Then he quickly grabbed the squealing, slippery pig and stuffed it into his fruit sack while the men all had their backs turned.

Seth took the bag and the boys proceeded to Chinatown, a narrow quadrangle of city blocks and alleys between Grant Avenue and Washington Street. Here they sold their loot in a Chinese washhouse for ninety cents, of which Rob was given only fifteen. He was satisfied, though; happy to know that once again he had conquered his fear. He was more and more convinced that his suspected cowardice was finally turning to courage.

Rob also had a brief interlude when he became a newspaper boy. His persistent pleading finally won his parents' reluctant permission to sell newspapers on the downtown streets of San Francisco. One of his friends in the Washington Street Gang taught him where and how to sell the papers. He learned quickly, and soon was shouting out the appealing headlines and searching for the customers most likely to buy from him. He learned, also, how to keep accurate records. Initially, he loved the challenge of the job and the grown-up feeling of earning his own money. But after just a few long, tiring days, when he realized that his profits were very small, he simply quit. He had learned early, when his mother approved his leaving school, that it was easy to quit. He would have to fight this tendency all his life.

Then it was the summer of 1884, and Rob's days were filled with campaigning with his father. This was the year that William had hoped to win the post of city tax collector. The dream was not to come true, though, and when he lost the election, his hopes for a political career were shattered. William Frost had never had the one or two lucky breaks that might have made it possible for a man of his ability to go on to become a high-ranking political figure. His brilliance in the worlds of journalism and politics was not enough to bring him the recognition he sought. Now the bitter disappointment was more than he could bear. For days he didn't come home. Finally, he arrived at

1404 Leavenworth Street in a drunken rage, a broken man. He never regained his spirit or his strength.

For the next few months William Frost was a silent and brooding stranger to his family. His illness seemed to be eating away at him. When he was home he drank his whiskey, but talked to no one. He ate his breakfast alone, then left for work without saying good-bye to his wife or children. When he returned home in the evening, he sat through dinner in silence.

The following spring, Rob and Jeanie, playing on the corner near their home one afternoon in May, had a vivid warning of what was to come. They saw their father being helped off a cable car, a blood-stained handkerchief held to his mouth. They watched in mute silence as their father's friend put his arm around the sick man and helped him walk the few steps down Leavenworth Street to their home. The arrival of the doctor, the hushed conversation, were enough to warn the children of the imminent tragedy.

That evening William called for Rob, and as the boy sat on his father's bed and listened, William whispered that he was never to go into the streets to play after dark. Rob never did.

The next morning, trying to keep busy and stay out of the way, the children were playing outside the house when a friend said, "There's crepe on your door." William P. Frost, Jr., was dead at the age of thirty-four. He had died in the arms of his old friend and political backer, Colin Boyd, a Scotsman. Ironically, his last request was that his body be taken back to New England for burial—back to the New England he had professed to hate. It was May 5, 1885, and Robert Lee Frost had just turned eleven.

The funeral service was conducted by the Reverend John Doughty, whose church William Frost would never enter when alive. Then Belle Moodie Frost discovered that her husband's twenty-thousand-dollar life insurance policy had lapsed because he had failed to make the payments. There was a little money in a bank account, but by the time the funeral expenses were paid there was only eight dollars left.

The senior Frosts sent enough money to pay for the train fare back to Massachusetts. As the forlorn little trio made their last journey across the bay on the ferry, Rob was probably thinking of the many happy times he had spent here with his father. They boarded the train in Oakland for the long and difficult journey "home."

Each time they changed trains, first in Omaha, Nebraska, and then in Chicago, Belle would leave the children for a few minutes, admonishing them to stay together, and go off by herself to check and recheck her husband's coffin. She was dressed in black, the only outward sign that she was bereaved, and she was still able to offer her children comfort and strength. They could not have known the torment raging within her. The acute loss of one who baffled and distressed her, yet whom she dearly loved; her fear of having to live with her husband's parents; her concern that they might blame her for the death of their only son; her lack of money to support herself and her children—all these were worries that filled her mind and her heart as they made the interminable journey east.

For Rob it was to mean an abrupt end to a life of freedom, and a loss that he would never be able to fully accept. Years later he would say, "I never spoke of my father for years after he went. I couldn't."

Birches

When I see birches bend to left and right
Across the lines of straighter darker trees,
I like to think some boy's been swinging them.
But swinging doesn't bend them down to stay
As ice storms do. Often you must have seen them
Loaded with ice a sunny winter morning
After a rain. They click upon themselves
As the breeze rises, and turn many-colored
As the stir cracks and crazes their enamel.
Soon the sun's warmth makes them shed crystal shells
Shattering and avalanching on the snow crust—
Such heaps of broken glass to sweep away
You'd think the inner dome of heaven had fallen.
They are dragged to the withered bracken by the load,
And they seem not to break; though once they are bowed
So low for long, they never right themselves:
You may see their trunks arching in the woods
Years afterwards, trailing their leaves on the ground
Like girls on hands and knees that throw their hair
Before them over their heads to dry in the sun.
But I was going to say when Truth broke in
With all her matter of fact about the ice storm,
I should prefer to have some boy bend them
As he went out and in to fetch the cows—
Some boy too far from town to learn baseball,
Whose only play was what he found himself,
Summer or winter, and could play alone.
One by one he subdued his father's trees
By riding them down over and over again
Until he took the stiffness out of them,

And not one but hung limp, not one was left
For him to conquer. He learned all there was
To learn about not launching out too soon
And so not carrying the tree away
Clear to the ground. He always kept his poise
To the top branches, climbing carefully
With the same pains you use to fill a cup
Up to the brim, and even above the brim.
Then he flung outward, feet first, with a swish,
Kicking his way down through the air to the ground.
So was I once myself a swinger of birches.
And so I dream of going back to be.
It's when I'm weary of considerations,
And life is too much like a pathless wood
Where your face burns and tickles with the cobwebs
Broken across it, and one eye is weeping
From a twig's having lashed across it open.
I'd like to get away from earth awhile
And then come back to it and begin over.
May no fate willfully misunderstand me
And half grant what I wish and snatch me away
Not to return. Earth's the right place for love:
I don't know where it's likely to go better.
I'd like to go by climbing a birch tree,
And climb black branches up a snow-white trunk
Toward heaven, till the tree could bear no more,
But dipped its top and set me down again.
That would be good both going and coming back.
One could do worse than be a swinger of birches.

· 3 ·

Too far from town to learn baseball

When the sad little band of three arrived in Lawrence, Massachusetts, they went straight to the senior Frosts' home on Haverhill Street, the main street in town. The more well-to-do members of the community, many of whom were native New Englanders, lived in houses on Haverhill Street. Most of the workers, though, were immigrants who lived in boardinghouses on Canal and Methuen streets. At that time Lawrence was well on its way to becoming the largest mill town in the East.

Number 370 Haverhill Street, their destination, was a white clapboard house, tall and unusually narrow. Rob, looking around him, was struck with the realization that the bright color of life as he had known it in San Francisco was being replaced by the dull gray of a New England mill town. The air seemed to be clogged with the gray smoke from the mills. He couldn't help but notice the difference in the quality of the light: the translucent light of San Francisco was gone. Removed from the openness of the harbor city of San Francisco, he suddenly felt closed in.

When they entered the house Rob stood close to his mother, not quite holding her hand, but trying to draw some strength from her at the same time that he wanted to offer her support. He hoped so much that he would be able to live up to the role she had told him he must now play, that of the man in the family.

At the entrance to the parlor Rob looked around apprehensively at the dimly lit room, full of heavy, dark furniture. Each couch and chair was covered to protect it from soiling. Suddenly, he was filled with a strange terror. Gathered in front of the fireplace, dressed in their best black, stood his father's relatives, a stiff, cold receiving line for the tired and emotionally drained travelers.

Grandfather Frost, tall and straight and unsmiling behind his carefully trimmed white beard and his silver-rimmed spectacles, was the first to greet them with a stiff handshake. Next to him stood Grandmother Frost, also stern and with not a hint of a smile. Then came Great-Uncle Elihu Colcord and Great-Aunt Lucy Colcord, and Great-Aunt Sarah Frost Messer.

If he were frightened when he first arrived, it didn't take Rob long to learn that his fears were not imaginary. Before they sat down to supper that night, Grandmother Frost sent the children to wash their hands and faces. Grandfather accompanied them to make sure they did a thorough job and didn't get the snowy white towels dirty. For Rob, accustomed to the independent life he had led in San Francisco, this was more humiliation than he could bear.

Nor did it end there. They were scolded constantly for tracking mud into the house, for leaving the screen door open, and for not coming to meals precisely on time. Rob and Jeanie, used to their mother's extreme leniency, found this intolerable.

They learned very quickly that in the textile mills in Lawrence the foreman's word was law. Their grandfather, who had been the foreman in one of the mills, seemed to have brought home with him his penchant for authority.

The life of the immigrant who worked in the Lawrence factories was regulated by the mill whistles. When the first one blew before six o'clock in the morning the Lawrence immigrant got out of bed. On the second whistle he marched into the factory. The final blast sent him home at night. William Frost expected to regulate the lives of his grandchildren in a similar manner.

Occasionally, on a rainy day, the children were allowed into their grandfather's woodshed, but were not permitted to touch his neat arrangement of garden tools and carpenter's tools. Once, when they mustered enough nerve to open the drawers of the workbench they found there, they discovered old newspapers, wrapping paper, cardboard, and folded paper bags, all stacked neatly in piles—being saved for possible use some day. In one tiny drawer they were startled to find old, used nails, all bent and rusty, but nevertheless arranged carefully according to size. They found also sheets of tin foil, carefully smoothed out, and little balls of string. Wide-eyed, they ran to their mother to tell her of their discovery. Belle tried to explain to them that Grandfather Frost was descended from the original "Yankees," tough-fibered people who set sail for an unknown land in protest against restrictions that were being placed on their personal freedom. They were determined and resourceful enough to build a flourishing farming, industrial, and cultural center in a new land. She explained that the Yankees very early developed the fine art of making the best of things, and of themselves. "Use it up, wear it out; make it do, or do without" became their motto.

Rob and Jeanie decided that Grandfather Frost was carrying this too far. Rob couldn't know then that this Yankee determination was later to play a major role in his poems and in his life.

Rob learned also that his grandfather was cruel. One day, as Rob watched from a window, he saw the old man hide behind the house, horsewhip in hand. Soon a little boy came into the yard and picked some flowers. Rob was horrified as he saw his grandfather spring out from his hiding place and lash the child's legs with his whip.

When Rob related the incident to his mother, she knew she could no longer expect the children to remain in this house. So she accepted the invitation of her late husband's uncle and aunt, Benjamin Messer and Sarah Frost Messer, to stay with them for a while in Amherst, New Hampshire. It was here that the children had their first taste of rural living. They were relatively happy here, free to roam the countryside after having been cooped up in the house on Haverhill Street for long months.

They enjoyed prowling through the meadows helping Uncle Messer gather wild blueberries and raspberries and riding into town in the wagon to sell them. On the farm Belle was happy to help Sarah can fruits and vegetables in glass jars for the winter.

By the time fall arrived, Belle thought it best to return to Lawrence so the children could attend school there. By borrowing some money from Uncle Elihu Colcord, she was able to rent two shabby rooms in an apartment house on lower Broadway.

The children took entrance examinations for school to determine

Haverhill Street was one of the loveliest streets in Lawrence, Massachusetts. Rob often walked here on his way to his grandparents' home from high school. *Courtesy Immigrant City Archives, Inc., Lawrence, Massachusetts.*

which grade they would enter. Rob was devastated when he learned that Jeanie would begin in fourth grade, while he must start in third. The exam had been unfair, he protested. He knew all about the West. Why did they ask him questions about the East? But he went to school, despite the indignity of being with eight-year-old "babies."

Rob and Jeanie managed to have fun, though, and nothing could spoil the excitement of their first snowstorm. They had never seen anything like it. It is probable that, in later years, Robert Frost identified so closely with New England and its changing weather because he had spent the first eleven years of his life in a relatively unchanging climate. His first snow was, therefore, all the more exciting for him.

Every aspect of the changing weather was a new discovery for him. One day, forced to stay indoors because of the cold, and having no friends to play with, Rob tried an experiment. He filled an old thimble of his mother's with water and placed it on the windowsill. Together he and Jeanie watched during the day as ice crystals began to form. The next morning, to their delight, they found a solid piece of ice inside. When he tapped it out onto the top of the stove, they were delighted to watch it dance about as it melted.

They were lonely, but they were already beginning to exhibit their Yankee heritage—their resilience of spirit in the face of adversity, their ability to "make do" with what they had. Years later Frost was to incorporate this into one of his best-loved poems. In "Birches" he described

> *Some boy too far from town to learn baseball,*
> *Whose only play was what he found himself,*
> *Summer or winter, and could play alone.*
> *One by one he subdued his father's trees*
> *By riding them down over and over again.*

They were all delighted when Henry George, their old friend from San Francisco, came to ease their loneliness. In New England on a lecture tour, he took time out to visit the Frosts and take them out for dinner, a rare treat.

Early in the winter of 1886 Belle Moodie Frost's courage and faith were finally rewarded. She was asked to fill a sudden vacancy as "upstairs" teacher of grades five through eight in District School Number Six in Salem, New Hampshire, only ten miles from Lawrence, just inside the New Hampshire border. The two-story school had one other teacher, the "downstairs" teacher, who taught grades one through four. Rob and Jeanie would both be in Belle's class.

Elated, Belle and the children moved to a lodging house across the railroad tracks at Salem Depot, which boasted a general store, two small shoe factories, a grain mill, a livery stable, two churches, about twenty houses, and the school.

Belle immediately began to put her theories of education into practice. As the widow of a Harvard graduate, and brought up by an uncle who had attended the University of Edinburgh, she was not about to accept the usual custom of allowing the children to complete eighth grade and then go to work. It was her idea that the brighter ones should be given an opportunity to go on to high school. She set about trying to inspire them to do so.

Belle used what were then considered new and original methods of teaching. She seated children according to their ability, taught them individually depending on their needs, and read aloud to them for some part of every day. Those students who did well sat at the back of the room, while those needing help or discipline were moved to the front.

Rob soon found that as his sister Jeanie was making steady progress toward the back of the room, he was moving forward. He still hated learning and refused to do some of the work. He much preferred whittling with his new jackknife, hiding what he was doing behind the large, open geography book he kept propped up on his desk.

It was at the Salem school that Rob first learned to play baseball, a sport he was to enjoy all his life. The older boys taught him to pitch. Then he developed the skill of batting, and finally realized one day that he could run the bases faster than most boys. He became a regular on the school team.

Before the spring term ended he had become friendly with a boy his age named Charley Peabody. Charley was full of mischief, but he was also a nature lover, and his room at home was filled with creatures he had caught. He had a hawk, an owl, two snakes, a flying squirrel, and a raccoon, all kept in screened boxes. On his walls was a collection of branches holding birds' nests, some even including eggs.

It was Charley who taught Rob how to climb birch trees and ride the branches down:

> *When I see birches bend to left and right*
> *Across the lines of straighter darker trees,*
> *I like to think some boy's been swinging them.*

He taught him how to track and trap animals, how to skin a woodchuck, and how to collect birds' nests.

That summer, though, Mrs. Frost decided that Rob was old enough to find a job and contribute some money to the family. Her salary as a schoolteacher was nine dollars a week for a school year of only thirty-six weeks, so it was important that Rob earn some money.

He was hired as an apprentice in a shoe factory, where all he did was hammer nails into the leather soles of shoes. Very soon, though, he was promoted to a much more difficult and important job. He was to be the assistant to the man who operated an automatic heel-nailing machine. The work was tiring and nerve-wracking, particularly because Rob knew that the boy who had the job before him had lost a finger while trying to straighten a misplaced nail.

Soon he thought up a scheme. He complained to his mother that the men at the factory used foul language, and even swore. His mother reacted as he had hoped she would. She insisted that Rob must not continue to remain in such a place. His ruse had worked.

Not long after, the Frosts grew tired of boardinghouse life, and moved into the farmhouse of Mr. and Mrs. Loren E. Bailey. The Baileys were a sympathetic Scottish couple who rented to the Frosts rooms and the use of the kitchen. For Rob, this was an opportunity to work again, and this time to enjoy it.

Loren Bailey had built a large shed behind his house, and he had several men working there cutting and assembling leather heels. The men worked to supplement their incomes, and Loren sold the finished products to some of the larger shoemaking companies near Boston. This was quite common at the time.

Soon Rob was given a chance to work there. Loren Bailey taught him how to hold the metal pattern, how to trace around it with a sharp cutting knife, and how to assemble, nail, and trim the pieces of leather. He was paid by the piece, so if he worked quickly he could make a lot of money. He had the added advantage of being able to listen to the conversations of the other farmers, wanderers, or tramps who happened to be working there, and this he loved.

Rob was troubled, though, by his mother. She seemed to be suffering from some kind of illness, although he never heard her complain. She looked thin, tired—even worn out—and there were deep hollows under her high cheekbones. She, who had always been so neat and careful of how she looked, so fastidious, now paid less and less attention to her clothes. Often her beautiful hair, streaked now with gray, would come undone from the bun at the back of her head. She seemed not to care at all. But she continued to find time at the end of every day, after teaching and doing all her chores at home, to read to Rob and Jeanie.

Rob's favorite story at that time was *Tom Brown's School Days,* and Belle read and reread it to him. He would not allow her to finish it, though. He told her he could not bear to think that such a good story could end. Perhaps Rob loved to hear about Tom because he was a boy of his own age—a runner, a fighter, a ballplayer—and proud of his skills. But Tom Brown was more than that. He was a good student, also. He was not ashamed to do schoolwork, and to study Latin and Greek. As Tom grew "in manfulness and thoughtfulness," Rob began to grow also.

He became more and more interested in reading and schoolwork.

Belle Frost's years of storytelling and of reading to him were beginning to pay off. Her trips from the Lawrence Public Library, her arms laden with books on Scottish history and folklore, were finally beginning to reap rewards.

Belle continued to expose Rob to good poetry as well. Her favorite poets were Wordsworth, Bryant, and Emerson, and she quoted them frequently. In fact, her repetition of Bryant's "To a Waterfowl" sank in so deeply that Rob suddenly realized one day, as he was cutting leather, that he was saying it to himself by heart.

Rob still did not read, though. He had never had to. His mother always read to him. It was Mrs. Bailey, the farmer's wife, who first induced him to read on his own.

One day, during the summer of 1887, when Rob was already fourteen years old, he and Mrs. Bailey were alone in the shed together, talking about their relatives in Scotland. Rob could easily match her story for story because he had been listening to his mother's tales for so long. But when Mrs. Bailey suggested that he borrow her copy of the historical novel *The Scottish Chiefs,* by Jane Porter, he was sufficiently intrigued to read it by himself.

He flopped down in the newly cut hay, and was soon lost in the history and romance of the Scottish Highlands. From then on he was a devoted reader. He began to work in school to catch up to the rest of his classmates. He knew that he would soon have to pass entrance examinations for Lawrence High School, and he knew also that Lawrence had an excellent baseball team. If he wanted to play on the team, he would have to be able to get good grades.

So he began to apply himself seriously to studying, but in his own way. He went through one subject at a time, passing his mother's examination at the end of each one, then going on to the next. He mastered geography first, then arithmetic, history of the United States, and grammar, and finally he read a literature anthology called *Higher Reader.* The grammar book had bored him, but he surprised himself by enjoying many of the stories and poetry in the *Reader,* even memorizing some of the poems.

When he finally took his entrance exams, he barely passed arithmetic, but he did so well on all the other tests that he was admitted. His sister Jeanie, two years younger, had passed easily.

HIGH SCHOOL BULLETIN.

"HONESTAS ET PERSEVERANTIA."

VOL. XI.   LAWRENCE, MASS., APRIL, 1890.   NO. 8.

THE SHEPHERD'S SONG.

'Tis the quiet evening,
When the sun sinks low,
And the birds and flowers
To their slumber go;
As the shadows deepen,
And the shades grow long,
Then the sturdy shepherd
Sings his evening song.

"In life's day so varied
All is for the best,
All day we may labour
But at last comes rest;
Though this world may trouble,
And its cares annoy,
In the land we hope for,
Comes eternal joy.

Never be discouraged,
Be both brave and strong
Till you rest in heaven—
It will not be long.
Let your work be joyful,
Hard though it may seem,
And through clouds of darkness
Light once more will gleam."

Then the moon arising
Spreads its mantle gray,
And the shepherd, singing,
Homeward hies his way.
And he sees the valley,
Calm and pure and white,
Glist'ning in the moonlight
Like a mirror bright.

C. J. C. '90.

LA NOCHE TRISTE.

TENOCHTITLAN.

Changed is the scene: the peace
And regal splendor which
Once that city knew are gone,
And war now reigns upon
That throng, who but
A week ago were all
Intent on joy supreme.
Cries of the wounded break
The stillness of the night,
Or challenge of the guard.
The Spaniard many days
Beseiged within the place,
Where kings did rule of old,
Now pressed by hunger by

The all-relentless foe,
Looks for some channel of
Escape. The night is dark;
Black clouds obscure the sky—
A dead calm lies o'er all.
The heart of one is firm,
His mind is constant still,
To all, his word is law,
Cortes his plan hath made,
The time hath come. Each one
His chosen place now takes,
There waits the signal, that
Will start the long retreat.

THE FLIGHT.

Anon the cry comes down the line,
The portals wide are swung,
A long dark line moves out the gate,
And now the flight's begun.

Aye, cautiously it moves at first,
As ship steered o'er the reef,
Looking for danger all unseen,
But which may bring to grief.

Straight for the causeway now they make,
The bridge is borne before,
'Tis ta'en and placed across the flood,
And all go trooping o'er.

Yet e'er the other side is reached,
Wafted along the wind,
The rolling of the snake-skin drum
Comes floating from behind.

And scarcely has its rolling ceased,
Than out upon the lake,
Where all was silence just before,
A conch the calm doth break.

What terror to each heart it bears,
That sound of ill portent,
Each gunner to escape now looks,
On safety all are bent.

Forward they press in wild despair,
On to the next canal,
Held on all sides by foe and sea,
Like deer within corral.

Now surging this way, now in that,
The mass sways to and fro,
The infidel around it sweeps—
Slowly the night doth go.

A war cry soundeth through the night,
The 'tzin! the 'tzin! is there,
His plume nods wildly o'er the scene,
Oh, Spaniard, now beware!

With gaping jaws the cannon stands,

Points it among the horde;
The valiant Leon waits beside,
Ready with match and sword.

The 'tzin quick springeth to his side,
His mace he hurls on high,
It crasheth through the Spanish steel,
And Leon prone doth lie.

Falling, he died beneath his gun,—
He died at duty's call,
And many falling on that night,
Dying, so died they all.

The faithful guarders at the bridge,
Have worked with might and main,
Nor can they move it from its place,
Swollen by damp of rain.

On through the darkness comes the cry,
The cry that all is lost;
Then e'en Cortes takes up the shout,
And o'er the host 'tis tossed.

Some place their safety in the stream,
But sink beneath the tide,
E'en others crossing on the dead,
Thus reach the other side.

Surrounded and alone he sits,
Upon his faithful steed;
Here Alvarado clears a space,
But none might share the deed—

For darkness of that murky night
Hides deeds of brightest fame,
Which in the ages yet to come,
Would light the hero's name.

His faithful charger now hath fall'n,
Pierced to the very heart.
Quick steps he back, his war cry shouts,
Then onward doth he dart.

Runs he, and leaping high in air,
Fixed does he seem a space,
One instant and the deed is done,
He standeth face to face—

With those who on the other side
Their safety now have found.
The thirst for vengeance satisfied,
The Aztec wheels around.

So, as the sun climbs up the sky,
And shoots his dawning rays,
The foe, as parted by his dart,
Each go their sep'rate ways.

Upon the ground the dead men lie,
Trampled midst gold and gore,
The Aztec toward his temple goes,

· 4 ·

And so, for us, the future rises

When Rob and Jeanie boarded the train at Salem Depot in September of 1888 to make the short trip to Lawrence High School together, Rob was wearing an old suit that had belonged to Grandfather Frost. Grandmother Frost had cut it down for him. His ticket was paid for by his grandparents as well.

While many of the people of Salem sneered at the "unnecessary" expense of going to school in Lawrence (most of the Salem youngsters who went to high school at all remained in Salem), the Frosts agreed that a good education at Lawrence High School, where Rob's father had gone, was important. Perhaps they were even beginning to think that Rob, too, might go on to Harvard.

Rob's first day at the high school was frightening and bewildering for him. The school, which stood on Haverhill Street not far from his grandparents' home, was a large and ugly brick building. Rob found that he was looked on as an outsider—a "country bumpkin" from Salem. But when he flipped through the well-worn textbooks in history, he became excited at the prospect of learning more about the heroes of Greece and Rome. He was able to forget, if only for a few moments, his fear of this new adventure.

Perhaps it was partly this fear that prompted him to work hard on his assignments at home. He didn't want to be embarrassed in front of his new classmates by not knowing the answers to questions put by his teachers. But the more he was driven to study, the more he found, to his surprise, that he enjoyed the work. More and more he found he loved to read—by himself—the myths, legends, and stories about Greece.

Lawrence High School, "an uncompromising brick building" on Haverhill Street that Rob and Jeanie attended. *Courtesy Immigrant City Archives, Inc., Lawrence, Massachusetts.*

And he found he loved Latin too, in spite of having to memorize declensions and conjugations. He suddenly understood why his mother had been diagramming English sentences on the blackboard, and what she meant when she talked about the Latin roots of words.

When *Vincit qui se vincit* was proposed as the motto for the class of 1892, he was able to guess the meaning before it was translated for him. More than that, he decided to adopt it as his own motto—"He conquers who conquers himself"—and to work hard to overcome his own laziness and fear.

By the time Rob had finished his first year at Lawrence High School, Great-Uncle Elihu Colcord had given him his first "boughten" suit as a reward for his outstanding success in school.

During the summer vacation of 1889, Loren Bailey asked Rob to help him harvest the crop on his farm. He taught him the intricacies of handling a grindstone, of swinging a scythe and keeping it "flat to the ground" to cut the sweet-smelling grass, and of using a pitchfork to catch huge bundles of hay and scatter them evenly in the mow. Rob had never worked harder, but he took pride in his newfound strength and in his ability to stay with the job and do it well. He was beginning to feel like a man.

When he returned to school as a sophomore in September, Rob

could feel the difference the past year had made in him. If he had not as yet completely overcome his shyness and his fear, at least now he was able to control them—and to hide the remainder under a pretense of arrogance.

Soon he made a new and somewhat unusual friend, a senior named Carl Burell. Carl was ten years older than Rob. He had not gone on to high school after eighth grade, but had worked as a laborer in a variety of jobs. When he decided to return to school to continue his education, he, like Rob, was looked upon by the other students as an outsider. No doubt the friendship of these two grew more out of shared loneliness than shared interests.

But Rob soon absorbed Carl's interests as his own. Carl had always been an amateur botanist, and from the time he was a little boy had loved to walk in the countryside searching for rare plants and flowers. These he would press, mount, and mark carefully. Rob soon found himself accompanying Carl on these walks, then borrowing and reading Carl's extensive collection of books on the subject. Their favorite plants then were ferns and orchids.

Much later Rob would pass this love for "botanizing" on to his own children, for it stayed with him for the rest of his life.

Rob was introduced to another subject through Carl. One day, browsing through Carl's library, he found a series of essays on the planets and the stars. He decided at once that he must own a telescope that would make it possible for him to see the rings around Saturn. When he came across an advertisement in a magazine, *The Youth's Companion,* offering a free telescope to anyone who sold a certain number of subscriptions to the magazine, Rob immediately set to work. Helped by his mother, who appealed to some of her friends, his house-to-house canvass eventually paid off. He won his telescope. Now he was even more anxious to read and learn about the wonders of astronomy. He became a familiar figure in the Lawrence Public Library, checking out books that described the names of the stars, the patterns of the constellations, and their positions at various times.

It may well have been Carl Burell also who inadvertently inspired Rob to try his hand at writing and publishing his own poetry. Carl had been a reporter on the monthly high school newspaper, the *Bulletin,* from 1887 until 1889. Rob had read many of Carl's poems and essays in the back issues of the *Bulletin* carefully stored on Carl's library shelves. Rob had never tried to work on it because he knew that the editors were generally English majors. He had chosen to follow the college preparatory, or classical program. Now, in history class, Rob was reading Prescott's *The Conquest of Mexico*. From this book he learned about the Aztecs, who had risen against their Spanish oppressors. He was stirred by the tales of these people, who had fought so desperately for their freedom, especially the Indians' victory on the night when they defeated the Spaniards in the city of Tenochtitlan, but he was saddened at their defeat there later by Cortez.

One bleak, windy March afternoon, as he was walking to his grandmother's house after school, as he often did, the Aztecs' story began going through his head. As he walked along, swinging his books in their strap, it suddenly began shaping itself into lines of poetry. The swinging books became a metronome, providing the rhythm of a ballad that he wanted.

As the stanzas kept coming to him, he became more and more excited. He was late getting to his grandmother's, but he went straight to the kitchen table, sat down, and began to write. He wrote twenty-five stanzas, without hesitation, just as he had conceived them in his head along the way. He called his ballad, appropriately, "La Noche Triste," "The Sad Night." Then he wrote a prologue of twenty-seven unrhymed lines and subtitled it "Tenochtitlan."

"It made very fast in my head," he would say seventy years later.

The next morning, excited yet nervous, he took his poem to school and left it on the desk of Ernest Jewell, chief editor of the *Bulletin,* before Ernest arrived. He was fearful that a poem written by a sophomore would not be published. But when the *Bulletin* appeared for April 1890, "La Noche Triste" was on the first page.

He was convinced now that he could write. He knew also that he would never do anything else. "I was lost when I wrote that first poem in ballad form."

Rob was so excited by his accomplishment that he soon wrote another poem, a lyric entitled "Song of the Wave." This was to be the first of many poetic references to his childhood in San Francisco. In "Song of the Wave" he recalled the twilight evenings with his family at Cliff House when they stood together taking in the sight and sound of the Pacific Ocean pounding on the rocks below. It was published in the May 1890 *Bulletin*.

After publication of his second poem in the *Bulletin*, a friendship began building between Rob and Ernest Jewell. Soon Rob, Ernest, and Carl were a familiar trio, involved together not only in the *Bulletin*, but in the debating club as well. And Rob was doing well in his studies also. He placed, as he had the year before, at the head of his class. Secretly, he derived much satisfaction from noting that some of his classmates who had originally treated him as the dumb country bumpkin from Salem were now looking at him with a newfound respect.

In his junior year Rob continued to concentrate on the classical studies program he had chosen when he first entered Lawrence High School. He knew, as he made his decision to continue studying Latin and Greek, that he was deliberately giving himself an exercise in self-discipline. But this was what he wanted. Moreover, he was fascinated by Latin verse forms. He found himself falling in love with poetry, with the sound of words.

When the time came for juniors to take preliminary examinations for college entrance, Rob was frightened at the prospect of taking seven hours of these exams at Harvard. But knowing that his father had attended Harvard, he assumed that, if the money could be found, he would go there also. So he set about preparing himself for the examinations in Greek, Latin, Greek history, Roman history, algebra, and geometry. He asked for a postponement, until the following fall, of the "prelim" in English literature. He felt he would not be able to read all the titles suggested by his English teacher by the spring. The postponement was granted, and when he traveled to Cambridge in March and then again in June, he passed all six exams. He passed the English literature exam in October.

As his junior year drew to a close, Rob was elated to find himself elected to the post of chief editor of the *Bulletin* for the following year. He immediately requested more help, and in the April issue of the *Bulletin* it was announced that in the future there would be seven instead of five literary editors.

In an early issue of the *Bulletin* during his senior year, Rob made a plea for more poetry, or more "verse" for the newspaper. While it did not accomplish its aim, it did reveal the earnestness of his concern with writing poetry.

Rob's interests were not restricted to his studies and poetry alone. His pride and insecurity had prevented him from attempting to win a place on the high school baseball team. He told himself, and the other students, that he didn't have time for practice because he had to commute to Salem and he needed his time for study. But he had lost none of his enthusiasm for sports.

Early in September, as he was casually watching the football team practice, he overheard one of the players say that someone was needed for scrimmage to give the first-string team adequate opposition. When someone else jokingly suggested that Rob Frost fill in, the mockery in his tone of voice was just sufficient to provoke Rob to accept. He peeled off his coat, put on a helmet, and took his assigned position. He played so well that he was immediately asked to join the team.

The next issue of the *Bulletin* contained the following article about the opening game against Bradford High School:

> No one would think that the man who played football on the right end was the same person who sits with spectacles astride his nose in the Chief Editor's Chair. Keep up the good work, Bobby.

He did. Lawrence High School was undefeated that season.

But he paid a price, one that none of his teammates guessed at. The ruthless and dangerous play always upset him, and he was sick to his stomach at the end of every game. In fact, after one particularly savage game, in which even his own speed, shrewdness, and flying tackles were more than he could bear, he walked off the field, knelt in the tall grass nearby, and vomited. He had made up his mind that the best way to overcome his fear was through courage and daring, and he continued to play.

❧

A source of delight for Robert in his senior year was a pretty young girl who sat next to him in his homeroom and whom he noticed casting shy, admiring glances at him. She was Elinor Miriam White, the dark-eyed daughter of a Universalist minister in Lawrence. Elinor, Rob soon found out, was enrolled in the general, or English program, rather than in the classical program as he was, and so the two had not met before. Also, he discovered, Elinor had been ill and had spent much time at home. She had a chronic disease called "slow fever," characterized by fever, weakness, and pain. Her fragile health would

LEFT: Robert Frost as senior class poet and valedictorian, Lawrence High School, 1892. *Courtesy Jones Library, Amherst.*

RIGHT: Elinor Miriam White shared honors with Rob as covaledictorian, Lawrence High School, 1892. *Courtesy Robin Hudnut.*

plague her all her life. She had, however, managed to keep up with her studies, and so would graduate on time with the class of '92.

Elinor, whose liberal father had recently deserted the pulpit to become a wood joiner, or cabinetmaker, was a true New Englander whose roots went all the way back to the Whites, who were among the first English settlers in America.

Rob soon found himself very much attracted to this lovely girl, and when she shyly submitted to him several poems, with the hope that he might see fit to publish one in the *Bulletin,* he promptly did.

A relationship began to form between them. Rob found that Elinor, in addition to being attractive, was also a match for his intellect and, therefore, a stimulating conversationalist.

He began to walk her home from school every day, carrying her books, and to take her to evening functions at the school. He even consulted her about editorial problems on the *Bulletin.*

Elinor seemed to know many more good poems than he did. Her wide reading on the history of English poetry prompted him to try to learn more about the subject. When he finally realized that he was truly in love with her, his first gift to her was two small books of poems written by Edward Rowland Sill, a New England poet who had died just a few years before, in 1887, at the age of forty-five. He found, soon after, that they shared also the love of another recent New England poet, Emily Dickinson.

Elinor continued to write poetry for about six months, but when her writing caused an argument with Rob, she apparently decided to give it up. In fact, years later, she even denied that she had ever written poetry at all. It would seem that a smooth and happy relationship with Rob was far more important to her than pursuing her own talents.

Rob soon found, though, that his love for Elinor was being put to the test. The principal of Lawrence High School called him to his office one morning to tell him that, at the moment, Rob appeared to have won the honor of being class valedictorian. He warned Rob, however, that there was a girl, albeit in the general program, who seemed to be a strong contender. The girl was Elinor White. Rob's initial delight was almost immediately replaced by jealousy. But his feelings for Elinor ultimately won out.

"Give the award to her," he told the principal. Mr. Goodwin declined. Finally, after much discussion, they agreed on a compromise. Mr. Frost and Miss White would be covaledictorians, but Rob would make the valedictory address to the class.

As it turned out, Elinor's final average was actually higher than Rob's. It is interesting to note that Rob was never able to deal with this satisfactorily. Years later, when one of his children jokingly referred to this fact in front of a visitor, Frost became enraged. He later ordered her never to tell the story again. Perhaps, had Elinor and Rob been growing up and attending school today, he would have been much better able to handle a situation in which the girl he loved was at least as bright as—or perhaps even brighter than—he was. Perhaps the entire course of their lives might have been different.

But then, the happy situation of being paired with Elinor as covaledictorians seemed to the young boy to be prophetic, and he determined that he would marry her. By the end of the term, before commencement exercises, they became secretly engaged.

Thursday, June 30, 1892—Commencement Day—dawned bright and beautiful. The annual graduation celebration in Lawrence was always an important and colorful one. The thirty-two members of the graduating class marched down the center aisle and up the steps to the stage. The class speakers were seated in the front row, with the town dignitaries. Rob, embarrassed at having to sit in the front row, was even more upset at the prospect of having to address all these people. He had carefully maneuvered in advance so that he would be seated at the end of the row. He hoped to be able to escape into the wings if he became too nervous waiting for his turn to speak. He also had been named Class Poet and his "Class Hymn," set to music by Beethoven, was to be sung at the conclusion of the ceremony. It ended:

> *And so, for us, the future rises,*
> *As thought-stones stir our heart's "Farewell!"*

At first he was able to concentrate on his speech, saying it over to himself, but as the other speeches dragged on, he became more and more upset. He was certain that he would forget his lines when he finally stood up to speak them. When he felt he could stand it no longer, he jumped up at the conclusion of a speech and ducked into the wings. He ran down the back stairs, found a sink, and soaked his handkerchief in the cold water. He wiped his face, head, and neck with it, then dried himself off on the sleeve of his jacket and quietly slipped back into his seat just as Elinor was finishing her talk. He knew that he was next. Trembling—almost overpowered by fright— he jumped up, walked quickly to the center of the stage, and rattled off his speech as quickly as he could. Its title, "A Monument to After-Thought Unveiled," reflected his recent discovery that his own best thoughts were always afterthoughts. Like the poet Wordsworth before him, he knew that his own most poetic insights, his most deeply felt perceptions, came when his emotions were recollected in tranquility.

> Not in the strife of action, is the leader made, nor in the face of crisis, but when all is over, when the mind is swift with keen regret, in the long after-thought. The after-thought of one action is the fore-thought of the next. The poet's insight is his after-thought.

And so he publicly paid tribute to the poetic career he had already decided to pursue.

But when his speech was finished, he found that his ordeal was not. Just as the applause subsided and he was back in his seat again, the superintendent of schools called him back to the center of the stage. He presented to Rob the Hood Prize, a small gold medal awarded for general excellence during his four years at Lawrence High School.

Reluctance

Out through the fields and the woods
    And over the walls I have wended;
I have climbed the hills of view
    And looked at the world, and descended;
I have come by the highway home,
    And lo, it is ended.

The leaves are all dead on the ground,
    Save those that the oak is keeping
To ravel them one by one
    And let them go scraping and creeping
Out over the crusted snow,
    When others are sleeping.

And the dead leaves lie huddled and still,
    No longer blown hither and thither;
The last lone aster is gone;
    The flowers of the witch hazel wither;
The heart is still aching to seek,
    But the feet question "Whither?"

Ah, when to the heart of man
    Was it ever less than a treason
To go with the drift of things,
    To yield with a grace to reason,
And bow and accept the end
    Of a love or a season?

· 5 ·

I have come by the highway home

Almost immediately after graduation Rob tried to convince Elinor to marry him. She, however, had every intention of going to college first, and was planning to leave for St. Lawrence University in upstate Canton, New York, at the end of the summer.

They spent a lovely, leisurely summer together, taking walks in the country, or going "upriver" in a little rowboat Rob had borrowed. They even exchanged rings secretly, conducting their own marriage ceremony. But Elinor refused to change her mind about school.

The summer ended all too soon. As Elinor prepared to leave for St. Lawrence, Rob decided that he might as well accept the scholarship that had been offered to him by Dartmouth College. His grandmother did not want him to attend Harvard, as he had originally expected, because she was convinced now that it was habits acquired at Harvard that had ruined her own son.

So, in September 1892, Rob boarded the train alone and rode to Norwich, Vermont, across the river from New Hampshire, and the beautiful Dartmouth College campus. When he arrived he found his rooms—a bare study and a small bedroom equipped only with a cot—on the top floor of Wentworth Hall. He immediately got into the swing of things, though, and was excited at the prospect of shopping for some secondhand furniture for his rooms. He even enjoyed the hazing of freshmen that was part of campus life. On his first night several boys opened his door and threw something into his room, upsetting his kerosene lantern, and leaving him in total darkness. Then they put enough screws into the outside of his door to hold it firmly closed. These were not removed until the morning.

"I thought this was all fun. It didn't worry me any. I thought this was what you came to college for," he said of this years later.

Rob soon made a good friend, a young man named Preston Shirley, from Andover, New Hampshire. The two built a fort in Preston's room, barricading the door with a closet door that they removed and braced against it with a wooden bed slat nailed to the floor. There they would eat the fruit and homemade candy that Preston's mother sent regularly. With the room set up like this, only one could go out at a time, so they cut classes alternately.

Both Rob and Preston were invited to join the fraternity Theta Delta Chi. When one of the wealthy brothers paid Rob's entrance fee, Rob's happiness should have been complete.

But it was not. He still longed for Elinor. He wanted her with him. Often he went for long, solitary walks in the surrounding countryside. He loved the area, and he loved having the opportunity to think by himself. He was still asking himself, Who am I? What will I do with my life? Why am I at college? When his fraternity brothers began to ask him mockingly what he did when he went off on his lonely walks, he flashed back, "I gnaw bark."

When winter arrived, it became necessary to keep wood or coal burning in the stove night and day in order to keep warm. But Rob was too lazy to clean the ashes out of the stove or carry them down to the dumping ground. He simply raked them onto the floor and let them pile up.

When he mentioned this jokingly to his mother in a letter to her, she prevailed upon Rob's old friend Carl Burell to visit him at school. The boys had a happy reunion, and Carl shoveled the room clean for his friend.

This was not the only area in which Rob was beginning to revert to his old habits of laziness. He was rapidly becoming bored with academic life. The only reading he seemed to be doing was an anthology of poems he had chanced upon in a campus bookstore entitled *The Golden Treasury of Songs and Lyrics,* by Francis Turner Palgrave. He spent hours reading from this the poems of Keats and Shelley, hours that should have been spent on homework assignments. It was a book that would come to have much meaning for him later, though. Its influence would last for the rest of his life. He found also, quite by accident, a magazine he had never seen before, the *Independent*. As he read the poem by an unknown (to him) American poet named Richard Hovey on the front page, and the editorial accompanying it, he began to wonder if he would ever write a poem worthy of publication on the front page of this periodical.

More and more he questioned the need for a formal education. He resented the students who placed such stress on grades, who studied solely for the marks they would earn at the end of the term rather than simply because they wanted to learn. In high school he had liked the A's he earned for the first three years. Toward the end of his senior year, though, he had begun to resent the strain of being talked about as the class leader. Now, at Dartmouth, he was beginning to feel the same way. He didn't want to talk about marks. It began to make him nervous. He was depressed, he was homesick, and he missed Elinor terribly.

When his mother, in one of her frequent letters to him, complained of the difficulty she was experiencing in disciplining some of her eighth-grade students, Rob had his excuse. He would quit school and return home to help his mother.

He confided his plans only to his friend Preston Shirley, and had one last late-night feast with him of candy and cookies. They carried on and said good-bye all night. Then Rob packed his bag and unceremoniously walked away from Dartmouth College and all it stood for. It was the first of many instinctive decisions to yield to his poetry. Perhaps, also, he felt that the situation at Dartmouth was unrealistic. To him, the greater integrity was in the leaving.

He did take over his mother's class for a short time (she was given another, lower grade to teach), and attempted to subdue the unruly boys by caning them with rattan sticks. He relinquished the job in late March, at the conclusion of the term.

Belle Moodie Frost never reproached her son for leaving Dartmouth. She seemed to understand his need to write poetry, and was content that he sought work to help support them. His grandparents, though, reacted differently. Grandfather Frost was hurt that a promising valedictorian to whom he had sincerely offered a college education should so disappoint him. Rob was looked on by the family as an obstinate, indecisive young fool.

&

Later that spring Elinor came home from college for a brief visit with her sister Ada, who was ill. Rob tried to persuade her not to return. They debated long and hard. Elinor, perhaps more mature than he, wondered how he could have given up his studies and be content to be idle. How could he betray the promises he had made as valedictorian? What did he see as their future? Would he be happy without a college education?

Rob retorted that she had changed, had come under bad influences at St. Lawrence. He had no plans—only a dream of someday becoming a famous poet. He could educate himself better than the Dartmouth professors could do it. He could earn money in many ways. He could teach school, work in a mill, do odd jobs.

Elinor protested that she would lose credit for her courses if she did not go back to school soon. She might have to repeat the entire freshman year. Rob insisted that he meant less to her than someone at St. Lawrence.

They argued and they argued. Finally, she sent word to school that she would not return until the fall. He knew he had won something, but Elinor's long silences, and his jealousy, made for an un-

Elinor White at St. Lawrence University, ca. 1895. *Courtesy Robin Hudnut.*

pleasant summer. When Elinor finally did return to St. Lawrence the following fall, Rob was lonelier than ever.

His memories of this summer, of the college student who hadn't made a go of it, who had not fit into the expected mold, are reflected in the poem "Bereft," published almost thirty-four years later. His distress at having no one understand him, at not being able to please anyone, not even himself, is evident here. He was lonely. He felt sorry for himself.

Leaves got up in a coil and hissed,
Blindly struck at my knee and missed.
Something sinister in the tone
Told me my secret must be known:
Word I was in the house alone
Somehow must have gotten abroad,
Word I was in my life alone
Word I had no one left but God.

Rob took a job as a light trimmer in the Arlington Woolen Mills. The mill was halfway between Methuen, where his mother had taken a position at another school, and Lawrence. His job necessitated his climbing a tall ladder, leaning over at a perilous angle, and reaching up to unfasten and replace the burned-out carbon filaments in the arc lamps. For this he was paid eight dollars a week. When the day was bright, and the lights not needed, Rob would climb up anyway to a hiding place he had found. Ignoring the whir of the turning wheel and the slapping of the leather belt as it went around, he read from a pocket-size volume of Shakespeare. Soon he found himself making notes in the margins of how he thought the passages should be spoken if they were to convey the real meanings. For the first time he became aware of the interplay between the rhythm of the metric line and the natural sounds of the spoken sentence. He studied Shakespeare for clues to help him understand these technical aspects of poetry to transfer to his own writing.

He made no real friends among the mill hands. In fact, several of the boys whom he had disciplined in his mother's school in Methuen were now working there, and soon found a way to reap their revenge for his harsh canings.

One winter evening, as he was walking home from work alone,

a group of the boys waylaid him, knocked him down, and punched and kicked at him. Fortunately for Rob, a passerby tried to stop them, all the while shouting for help. The tormentors ran.

But Rob had been humiliated—as well as badly beaten. When he stood up he saw two of his old classmates from Lawrence High School. They had obviously witnessed the entire scene. Rob could tell that they were disgusted that a class valedictorian could have degenerated so soon into a mill hand and a street fighter. What had happened to the "pride of Lawrence"? Where was the bright promise of high school?

At the same time Rob's mother was having her own difficulties. Unable to handle the disciplinary problems in her classes, she was finally relieved of her teaching duties. The loss of her salary made it necessary for the Frosts to give up their comfortable apartment in Methuen and move to a shabby tenement in Lawrence.

As Rob's situation grew steadily worse, Elinor seemed to be thriving. She was mingling with the bright and wealthy young men from St. Lawrence, and enjoying herself thoroughly. Rob was hurt and dejected. Would he ever make a name for himself as a poet? He was beginning to doubt that he could.

One aspect of his situation was resolved for him, in part as a result of an old fault of his—his habit of oversleeping in the morning. As Rob approached the mill one dreary winter morning, he heard the sound of the mill bell and knew that the gate was about to close. He ran, but it clanged shut just as he reached it, and he was left standing outside. He stood for a moment, frustrated, then shouted, "You can't do this to me," turned his back to the gate, and walked away. He never returned.

Rob knew that he had to do something or he might lose Elinor too. So he quickly found a job teaching elementary school in a tiny district school in South Salem. This, he discovered, he enjoyed doing. He loved working with the children, and he frankly enjoyed the respect afforded him by them and their parents.

Shy, lonely, headstrong, he seemed to be drifting along. But he had a feeling that his laziness meant something. He had a force within him that seemed to direct him to pursue his poetry.

One Sunday evening he locked himself in the kitchen, the warmest room in the apartment, sat down at the table, and began to write a poem. It was inspired by the memory of a fragile butterfly wing he had found lying among some dead leaves during the autumn he had spent at Dartmouth.

"I wrote it all in one go, in the kitchen of our house in Tremont Street," he said much later. "I locked the door and all the time I was working, Jeanie, my sister, tried to batter it down and get in." He ignored her, and didn't open the door until he had finished the poem. "As I wrote, I sensed in a way that something was happening. It was like cutting along a nerve. It was the beginning of *me*."

He called the poem "My Butterfly: An Elegy." As he reread the lines he had written, he knew for the first time that he had caught poetic qualities that seemed beyond his reach. He cried with joy.

Rob sent the manuscript off to the *Independent,* the magazine he had chanced upon at Dartmouth. Much to his surprise—and delight— it was accepted quickly by William Hayes Ward, the editor, and a check for fifteen dollars sent to Rob. He was a published author! Miss Susan Hayes Ward, sister of the editor, wrote to Rob both praising and criticizing his efforts, and so began the first step in a wonderful and creative friendship.

Miss Ward had a warm heart and a bright intellect, and her interest in Rob and his poetry came at a time when he desperately needed critical advice and recognition. He was grateful for her letter, and responded by promising to heed her advice that he improve his spelling. He then went on to tell her of "the astonishing magnitude of my ambition." He was more determined than ever now that he would be a poet.

When Mr. Nathaniel Goodwin, principal of Lawrence High School, heard of Rob's accomplishment, he invited him to his home and suggested that he would be happy to help Rob secure a job as a newspaper reporter. Rob thanked the man, but told him that was not exactly what he wanted to do. When Mr. Goodwin, annoyed, suggested that perhaps Rob thought the world owed him a living, Rob said no, but he would like to think the world would allow him to earn a living at whatever he could do best.

❧

When Elinor returned home from St. Lawrence just a few months later, Rob tried to persuade her to marry him. She refused, telling him that she must finish college, and that she couldn't marry him until he had found a job and could support them both. Then she went off to Boston for the summer, to work for a composer.

When she finally returned home, near the end of the summer, Rob went to visit her. But she wouldn't let him in. The president of her college was there.

"He thought I was a fool. I must have looked awful to Elinor. I looked worse than unpromising. Everybody was broken up by the way I *looked*. I had no sense of being defiant—I just went this vague way."

Rob begged Elinor to have faith in him and in his ability to write poetry. But Elinor White wanted a college education, and she wouldn't marry him until she had completed it. In the fall she returned to school. She did relent a little, though, and promised to accelerate her studies and graduate one year ahead of schedule. She promised Rob that if he had a responsible job by the time she graduated, in June 1895, she would marry him. Rob was still not satisfied.

Unable to settle on anything, Rob continued to drift listlessly from one odd job to another. Finally, his grandfather, heartbroken that his grandson, who had shown such promise of achieving great things, was floundering, tried to talk to him. He told Rob how proud he was that Rob had sold a poem to the *Independent*. He told him that he understood how his need to write was preventing him from pursuing a profession. Then he offered to support him for a year in order to allow him to write poetry. The only condition he asked was that if, at the end of the year Rob had not made a financial success of his writing, he would give it up.

Rob, instead of gratefully accepting or declining the offer, stood up, assumed the pose of an auctioneer, and chanted, "I have one, who'll give me twenty? One give me twenty—twenty-twenty-twenty." While he was still chanting, his grandfather walked out of the room. He could not have known then that it would, indeed, be twenty years before he would have his first book of poems published.

❧

In the fall of 1894 Rob made a last attempt to prove to Elinor that he could truly earn a living for both of them by writing poetry. He chose four poems he had written, each with a reference to some shared experience with Elinor, and took these, along with "My Butterfly," to a printer in Lawrence. Here, at his own expense, he had two copies of each poem printed on antique paper and bound in brown pebble leather. The title, *Twilight,* taken from one of the poems, was to be stamped in gold on the cover. One book would be for him, one for Elinor, a subtle declaration of his love for her, and proof, he hoped, that he was not a failure.

Encouraged by Elinor's mother, Rob decided to deliver the book to Elinor himself. Mrs. White gave Rob the money for his railroad ticket to Canton, helped him select a new suit, and even accompanied him to the railroad station to see him off.

The ride from Lawrence to Canton was a long one. It was an overnight journey, and Rob sat up in the coach through the night thinking of how Elinor would receive him and what the venture might mean for both of them.

When the train arrived early the next morning, Rob, his heart pounding at the prospect of seeing Elinor, walked to the campus of St. Lawrence, found his way to the house where Elinor lived, and excitedly knocked on the door.

But Rob did not know that it was against the rules then for girls to have visitors at any but specific evening hours. So when Elinor looked at him with a mixture of distress and reproach in her eyes, he misunderstood her meaning. When she calmly took the book from him, told him she would speak to him when she returned to Lawrence, and firmly closed the door, Rob was devastated.

Blindly he stumbled away from the house and started walking down the railroad tracks toward home. Overcome by grief, by frustration, by anger, he pulled his own volume of poems out of his pocket, ripped the pages out of the binding, and tore them to shreds. Then he took the next train home.

Just a short time later, receiving no encouraging word from Elinor, overwrought with jealousy, hurt pride, and utter discouragement, he impulsively decided to run away. Determined to hurt those who cared about him, perhaps even to commit suicide, he packed a bag and left home, telling no one where he was going.

He ended up in Norfolk, Virginia, near the Dismal Swamp. "I

was trying to throw my life away," Rob explained it in later life.

The Dismal Swamp was a swamp-forest that looked like wilderness. Its thick underbrush was shelter for dangerous wild animals, and the areas of dry ground often contained rattlesnakes. Rob knew this as he walked from Norfolk toward the swamp. But he continued, even after dark, until he finally reached it. His old fears of the dark should have been enough to keep him out. But there seemed to be something pushing him ahead, some force driving him forward—a force strong enough to overcome his fears and to allow him to keep on walking through the swamp for almost ten miles. It was near midnight when he finally saw light at the other end.

Rob continued his wanderings for three weeks, eventually jumping on a freight train bound for Washington, D.C., and hiding in a boxcar corner for hours. By the time he arrived in Washington he was so frightened, tired, and hungry that he asked a policeman if there were any chance he could be locked up in a jail for the night. There was, the policeman replied, and told him exactly where and how to go about it. Years later, Rob loved to tell the story of how he had spent his first night in Washington in jail.

Finally, not able to earn enough money for food, utterly exhausted, lonely, and homesick, and apparently not really interested in committing suicide, Rob swallowed his pride and wrote to his mother asking for train fare to come home. On Friday, November 30, 1894, he arrived back in Lawrence.

He found that while he had been gone—on November 8, 1894—his poem "My Butterfly: An Elegy" had appeared on the front page of the *Independent*. Rob immediately sent a letter to Miss Ward, then wrote another poem, entitled "Reluctance," expressing his sadness and his lost hopes. It began:

> Out through the fields and the woods
>   And over the walls I have wended;
> I have climbed the hills of view
>   And looked at the world, and descended;
> I have come by the highway home,
>   And lo, it is ended.

The Independent.

Entered at the Post Office at New York, as Second-Class Mail Matter.

"EVEN AS WE HAVE BEEN APPROVED OF GOD TO BE INTRUSTED WITH THE GOSPEL, SO WE SPEAK; NOT AS PLEASING MEN, BUT GOD WHICH PROVETH OUR HEARTS."

VOLUME XLVI.   NEW YORK, THURSDAY, NOVEMBER 8, 1894.   **NUMBER 2397.**

For Table of Contents see Page 10.

MY BUTTERFLY.

AN ELEGY.

BY ROBERT LEE FROST.

Thine emulous, fond flowers are dead too,
  And the daft sun-assaulter, he
That frighted thee so oft, is fled or dead :
    Save only me
    (Nor is it sad to thee),
    Save only me
There is none left to mourn thee in the fields.

The gray grass is scarce dappled with the snow ;
  Its two banks have not shut upon the river ;
    But it is long ago,
  It seems forever,
  Since first I saw thee glance,
  With all the dazzling other ones,
    In airy dalliance,
  Precipitate in love,
Tossed, tangled, whirled and whirled above,
  Like a limp rose-wreath in a fairy dance.

When that was, the soft mist
  Of my two tears hung not on all the fields,
  And I was glad for thee,
  And glad for me, I wist.

And didst thou think, who tottered wandering on high,
And fate had not made thee for the pleasure of the wind,
  With those great, careless wings,
  'Twas happier to die
  And let the lay. blow by.
  These were the unlearned things.

It seemed God let thee flutter from his gentle clasp,
  Then, fearful he had let thee win
  Too far beyond him to be gathered in,
Snatched thee, o'er-eager, with ungentle grasp,
  Jealous of immortality.

Ah, I remember me
How once conspiracy was rife
Against my life
  (The languor of it !), and
Surging, the grasses dizzied me of thought,
  The breeze three odors brought,
  And a gem flower waved in a wand.
Then, when I was distraught
  And could not speak,
Sidelong, full on my cheek,
What should that reckless zephyr fling
But the wild touch of your dye-dusty wing !

I found that wing withered to-day ;
  For you are dead, I said,
And the strange birds say.
  I found it with the withered leaves
  Under the eaves.

LAWRENCE, Mass.

AT THE END.

BY DANSKE DANDRIDGE.

Fearlessly into the Unknown
Go forth, thou little soul.
Launch out upon the trackless sea,
Nor wind nor stars to pilot thee.
  Alone, alone, alone !

Thine is a helpless plight.
Thou canst not turn thy helm,
Nor reach the harbor any more :

OUTLINES.

BY ELIZABETH C. CARDOZO.

I.—BEFORE THE MERCY-SEAT.

I dreamt that I stood, a naked soul, before the throne of God. And he questioned me, saying : What hast thou done with thy innocence, that fine white garment wherewith I clothed thee ?

I answered in bitter shame : I have trod the paths and breathed the airs whereby is innocence crushed. The mire of humanity is upon me.

And God said : What hast thou done with thy courage, that stout shield wherewith I did provide thee ?

I answered, bowed unto the ground : Alas, my shield is rent in twain, for it hath indeed been mercilessly battered.

And God said : What hast thou done with thy reason, that keen sword wherewith I did arm thee ?

I answered, overwhelmed with shame : The miasmas of the slums breathed upon it, and the sight of misery blinded it, and the voice of unheeded wrong thundered upon it, so that I am clean bereft thereof.

And God said : What hast thou done with thy love, that bright halo wherewith I did crown thee ?

I answered, with bowed head : I have so squandered it upon thy creatures that I know not if the remnant be a fitting gift to lay at thy feet. And I stretched out my empty hands.

And God said : What is that in thy hands that shines so fine gold ?

And behold, it was human love.

II.—THE CHOICE.

Before my soul had yet endured the pangs of human life, God showed me the earth.

And I beheld a marvelous fair country whereon were lofty mountains and stately edifices, the last being the work of the hands of man.

And I said : The world is very fair, I fear not to be born therein.

God said unto me : Look thou closer.

And behold, when I looked more closely, I saw that there ran hither and thither, over the face of this fair world, a mighty throng of creatures that never rested, but sought perpetually each to destroy the other. Only a few were quiet, and these were speedily overcome.

I asked : What race is this ?

And God said unto me : This is man.

I asked : What doth he unto his brothers ?

And God said : He preyeth upon him. Behold I have shown thee this that thou mayest choose. I send thee into this world that thou seest. Wilt thou be of them that destroy or wilt thou be the prey ?

I answered : I will be the prey.

Pity me not, my brothers, in that I am destitute of the good things of this earth, for I have chosen.

NEW YORK CITY.

REMINISCENCES OF MR. GLADSTONE.

AN INTERVIEW WITH DR. NEWMAN HALL.

It was in his charming house, close by the Heath, that I found Dr. Hall a few days ago, just returned from a busy week of preaching in the country. Dr. Hall travels far and wide, often preaching five and six times a week ; but his mind must often wander back to "Vine House," with its pretty garden, and its walls covered with clustering vines. Seventy years have passed over his head, and yet he told me four days ago he went for a sixteen-mile walk, and climbed a mountain nearly three thousand feet high without fatigue. "And I never feel Mondayish," he exclaimed. Indeed, there was something in his physical vigor akin to that of his great contemporary, Mr. Gladstone, who is only seven years his senior, and of whom he speaks in terms of great admiration.

"I have known Mr. Gladstone for twenty-five years," said Dr. Newman Hall. "He has spent several evenings

---

Mr. Gladstone. I do not agree with his Home Rule policy, because I keep to what he taught six years ago. I have not changed ; it is he who has changed his idea of carrying it out. But his kindness has in no degree diminished because of our difference of opinion on that point. He once said to me : ' I am sorry that you and Spurgeon, Dr. Dale and Dr. Allon do not see as I do.' I replied in substance that perhaps we might all agree better with one another if we all understood better what it is which we individually do really see. It is a mistake to suppose that I object to Home Rule altogether because I object to a particular method. I consider that all matters relating to local interests should be settled in the locality, and not brought to Westminster. Thus there should be Home Administration for Ireland, Wales, Scotland, England alike—neither more nor less ; but the Union should remain, in regard to all united and Imperial interests, untouched.

"I am indignant at some of the spiteful things said of him and evil motives attributed, because of differences of political opinion. At the last but one Handel festival, when Mr. and Mrs. Gladstone went out during the interval, I saw two ladies, very fashionably dressed, go up behind him, one of whom hissed in his ear. I was some distance off, by reason of the crowd. On returning to hear the second part of the oratorio, I heard a lady say : ' Didn't I hiss in his ear !' I turned round and saw the same two ladies, and could not forbear saying, in a loud voice : ' And you ought to be ashamed of yourself. We may not agree with Mr. Gladstone in politics, but we ought to honor him as one of the greatest men of the day, who has spent a long life in the service of his country.' The so-called ' ladies' seemed somewhat crestfallen.

"By the way," added the doctor, "one day I saw Mr. Gladstone at Dr. Allon's church, listening to Dr. Dale ; he also came to Christ Church on one Sunday evening when I was preaching.

"The other day when he was at Dollis Hill, waiting for the operation on his eye, I went to call on him. But he sent a kind message to say that by doctor's orders no one could see him, and he was very sorry that the rule could not be broken. I had, however, brought his last photograph with me, so I asked whether it would be possible for him to write his autograph on it. The photograph was taken up to him, and came back almost immediately with his signature appended. It has a prominent place in the doctor's study.

"About two years ago I also met Mr. Gladstone at Barmouth. Hearing that he was coming there, I went to the station to meet him. I was the first he greeted, and I think the only one whom he knew. I carried to the station a large bouquet of heather, which I gave to Mrs. Gladstone, saying : ' The Welsh hills greet you !' A large crowd followed him to his hotel, where he gave a short speech, while Mrs. Gladstone occasionally waved the bunch of heather.

"Mr. and Mrs. Gladstone once asked me to bring the Negro Jubilee Singers to their house to breakfast, and I took breakfast with them. The Gladstones had also invited some dozen aristocratic people, and the Jubilee Singers were sandwiched between them, and not placed all together ; so that you saw in one place a well-known countess, and by her side a full-blown Negress, all waited upon in an equal way. Mr. Gladstone engaged in conversation on matters of interest to them, and showed a wonderful knowledge of Negro character and history. After breakfast the singers sang for about an hour. Mr. Gladstone sat on the sofa, and his eyes were moist with emotion, while he seemed absorbed in the music. In the next morning's paper I saw that he went by special train at twelve o'clock to see the Queen at Windsor, and on the same afternoon made a great speech in the House of Commons. That was a very important and busy day, yet it commenced in the way I have told you.

"He might well write as he does here," continued Dr. Hall, turning to a letter from Mr. Gladstone—' My daily

Flower-Gathering

I left you in the morning,
And in the morning glow
You walked a way beside me
To make me sad to go.
Do you know me in the gloaming,
Gaunt and dusty gray with roaming?
Are you dumb because you know me not,
Or dumb because you know?

All for me? And not a question
For the faded flowers gay
That could take me from beside you
For the ages of a day?
They are yours, and be the measure
Of their worth for you to treasure,
The measure of the little while
That I've been long away.

° 6 °

The little while that I've been long away

The following month, when Elinor came home for Christmas, there was one terrible, stormy scene, one to match the stormiest December weather. In the heat of the argument Elinor returned the gold ring Rob had given her in secret two years before. He flung it into the fire in the coal range in the kitchen. She retrieved it. When the storm subsided, Elinor and Rob were officially engaged to be married. From this day on Elinor seemed to accept the force of poetry in Rob's life and never faltered in her support.

Shortly before this, Belle Frost had opened a private school in Lawrence, struggling courageously for her own brand of personal expression. The school was in an office building on Essex Street, near the center of the city. She rented two rooms for her school, and two more for living quarters. Jeanie was her assistant.

Rob and Elinor were married in this schoolroom on December 19, 1895. Since Elinor's father disapproved of the match, he would not permit the wedding to be held in his home. Nor would he attend. Neither Elinor nor Rob had any church affiliation, so they would not be married in a church. But the office-classroom had been used as a meeting place for the Swedenborgians in Lawrence, and the Reverend John A. Hayes of Salem, Massachusetts, a longtime friend of the Frosts, was happy to perform the ceremony there.

As they stood together before Reverend Hayes, exchanging vows, it is possible to assume that Elinor was thinking she loved this young man so much that she would help him succeed as a poet. She seems to have known, too, that to do this she would have to sacrifice much.

Elinor had always reached for the unusual—for a cause to champion. She was bright, talented—she wrote poetry herself, she painted. She must have sensed that she would not be able to pursue either of these talents, but she knew also that Rob's love for her was strong and deep, and this would be enough.

The young couple moved in with Mrs. Frost and Jeanie after the wedding, postponing a honeymoon until the end of the school year. The four shared home, money, and teaching duties, working hard to make a financial and educational success of the little school.

There were approximately twenty students, and one of them, who attended the school for the six years it existed, Clara Searle (Mrs. H. K. Painter), recalled the blackboard above the fireplace on which poems were written every day. The children copied these into their notebooks and learned them by heart. She remembered also the arithmetic class at the back of the room, near the door to the family dining room. She described the expectant hush as the students waited each morning for the door to open and the blue-eyed young man to come in to teach them. The aroma of toast still associates itself in her mind with arithmetic.

"I have known and learned from many inspiring teachers," she has said, "but the four who made that school are by themselves apart. Holding them together, holding the school together, calmly, quietly, with the light of humor in her eyes, stands that simple, careless, spare figure, beloved of the little child." From this beloved teacher, Robert Frost's mother, the poet surely must have drawn inspiration and developed later his own methods as a teacher. Belle Frost "treated every child as an individual, used no obvious discipline, and gave rewards that introduced the child into the world of literature." In later years Rob would dedicate a book of poems for children to this memory of his mother.

TO BELLE MOODIE FROST
Who Knew As A Teacher
That No Poetry Was Good For
Children That Wasn't Equally
Good For Their Elders

But Rob was not satisfied. Poetry was still pulling at him. The conflict within him continued to grow. He had to write. He knew he could write, and teaching was drawing him away from it.

Very soon this conflict began to take its toll on him physically. He was plagued by severe pains in his stomach and his solar plexus (the nerves behind the stomach), and he found himself waking up in the middle of the night perspiring and feeling as though he had a fever. The doctor diagnosed it as acute nervous tension.

And there were many tensions building up. His mother had become ill, his teaching duties were increasing and placing demands on his nervous energies, the living arrangements were not adequate for the four of them, and the financial strain was becoming unbearable. He was also beginning to feel guilty about Elinor. Had he let her down? Had he failed to keep faith with her? How could he support them all—and write his poetry too? Elinor, for her part, asked for nothing. She read every poem Rob wrote. That was her joy.

By the time the school term ended, Rob collapsed. He slept day and night for an entire week. Then, rested, he wrote:

> *I slept all day,*
> *The birds do thus*
> *That sing a while*
> *At eve for us.*
>
> *To have you soon*
> *I gave away—*
> *Well satisfied*
> *To give—a day.*
>
> *Life's not so short*
> *I care to keep*
> *The unhappy days;*
> *I choose to sleep.*

He titled the poem "The Birds Do Thus," and sent it to Susan Ward. She bought it and published it in the *Independent*. Then he made plans to take Elinor on a delayed honeymoon.

They asked Carl Burell, their old friend from Lawrence High

School, to help them find a cottage to rent in the country. This he did—in the village of Allenstown, New Hampshire, near the Suncook River.

Before Rob and Elinor arrived, Carl planted flowers around the house and started a kitchen garden of lettuce, tomatoes, onions, peas, and string beans for his friends. The original interest in "botanizing" that Rob had absorbed from Carl years before was about to be reawakened.

Carl's enthusiasm was easily transferred to Rob and to Elinor. They delighted in the specimens of plants he gathered along the road between the boardinghouse where he was living and their cottage. He told them stories about the color and structure and fragrance of flowers, and soon had Rob borrowing his books on botany, reading them avidly, then taking long walks to look for specimens himself.

At first Elinor accompanied him on these walks. As the summer wore on, though, she found herself more inclined to rest than to walk. She was, by then, seven months pregnant. She encouraged Rob to go without her, often napping while he was gone. When he stayed away longer than expected the old feeling of guilt would return—particularly when Elinor characteristically said nothing to reproach him. His tender love poem "Flower-Gathering" was written as an apology to her:

> *I left you in the morning,*
> *And in the morning glow*
> *You walked a way beside me*
> *To make me sad to go.*

Rob and Elinor's first child, a son named Elliott, was born on September 25, 1896. The next year they rented an old house at Salisbury Point, in Amesbury, Massachusetts, and tried to decide what to do.

Alone in the attic one day, reading a Latin text by the historian Tacitus and wondering how he could earn a living for his wife and his little son, Rob suddenly thought, Why can't I go to college and become a teacher? He thought he might teach Latin and Greek on a high-school level.

Still clutching the book, Rob ran downstairs to where Elinor was bathing ten-month-old Elliott in the kitchen, and excitedly told her his idea. She seemed indifferent—in fact, she said nothing—and Rob felt a chill go through him. He was hurt by her lack of interest, by the fear that she had lost all hope for his future. The guilt he often felt—at his unfairness to her, at his inability to provide for a wife and child—flashed through him now once again. What could he do? How could he change? Would she understand that this desire to go back to school implied that he was ready to take on responsibility—to prepare himself for a new way of life?

On September 11, 1897, Rob wrote a letter to Dean Briggs of Harvard requesting admission. This was granted provided he pass a group of entrance examinations in Greek, Latin, ancient history, English, French, and physical science (astronomy and physics). Rob had never taken courses in French or physics, but he knew what to do. He had studied Elinor's French books while she was teaching French in his mother's school, so he prevailed upon her to help him strengthen his knowledge of verb conjugations. His ongoing interest in astronomy had kept him reading in that area, so he had some background there. As for physics, he simply located a high-school textbook on the subject and read it through. The challenge excited him, and he was happier than he had been in a long time. He passed all the exams.

Grandfather Frost agreed to pay his tuition, Elinor's mother rented a house for them in Boston, and Rob enrolled as a freshman. He took Greek, Latin, philosophy, and the required freshman English. This last he hated—he found he was too mature for a beginning course—and when he handed in a poem he had previously written, "Now Close the Window," in place of an assignment, he antagonized the professor.

He loved the classical verse he learned in his Greek class, though, and did so well in it that he won the Detur, an honor Harvard bestows in the classics. This love of the classics was to stay with him all his life and enable him to bring to his own poetry a knowledge of Greek and Latin writers unsurpassed by any other American poet. He was even able to refer to them casually—but accurately—in conversation.

When he read Virgil's *Eclogues* and *Georgics* in the original, he had the nourishment he craved. "I first heard the voice from a printed page in a Virgilian eclogue and from *Hamlet*," he would say much later. He thought back to the time when, as a light trimmer in the Arlington Mill, he would read from his pocket Shakespeare high above the machines. Then, too, he had "heard" the poetry spoken.

"Poetry has to do something to you with sound. I do not care about meaning except as I use it to get meaning out of tone of voice," he said years later, in 1935. From his Harvard days on, his writing consisted mainly of "images to the ear."

Now Rob listened with delight to George Lyman Kittredge reading the poetry of Milton. He stored up images for future use as metaphors from the lectures of Nathaniel Southgate Shaler on historical geology. He loved learning, but he was still not happy.

He had made very few friends at Harvard. He was shy, and a married freshman was unusual. In addition to attending classes and doing the necessary reading and preparations, he had taken a part-time job in a Cambridge public school to earn some money for his family. He also found himself traveling more and more frequently to Lawrence to help his mother with her school. She was growing steadily weaker and was not able to run the school with only Jeanie to assist her. And Elinor needed him more at home. She was expecting their second child, and Rob often had to shop, prepare meals, and care for little Elliott. He was restless, he didn't seem to like things at school again, and then, as a final blow, the pains in his solar plexus returned.

Fearing that he might have tuberculosis (as his father had), he made up his mind to withdraw from Harvard. This time, though, he did not leave without telling anyone the way he had at Dartmouth. He spoke to Dean Briggs. The Dean expressed sorrow that Frost was leaving, and insisted on giving the young man a letter of reference attesting to his excellent record at Harvard. Rob left Harvard on March 31, 1899. On April 28 his daughter Lesley was born in Boston.

When Elinor was strong enough to return to Lawrence, Rob finally consulted their family physician. The doctor advised that Rob change his entire way of life by eliminating the nervous strain of teaching and engaging in physical activity out-of-doors.

So the young couple, with two tiny children, went to raise chickens in Methuen, about three miles from Lawrence. They settled in happily. Rob even enjoyed building shelters for the incubators in which the eggs were to hatch and, in his spare time, looking for orchids in the surrounding lowlands.

But their happiness was short-lived. They soon realized that Belle Frost was dying of cancer. They took her to live with them. She accepted her fate with the same quiet courage she had always shown and delighted in helping Elinor care for the children. Her particular joy was blond, blue-eyed Elliott, not quite four years old, who returned his grandmother's love full measure.

Then, in July 1900, Elliott suddenly became ill. By the time the doctor was called, he had become much worse. The doctor, annoyed at not having been called immediately, bluntly told the parents: "This is cholera infantum. It's too late, now, for me to do anything. The child will be dead before morning."

Elliott died that night. His parents were inconsolable. Their grief seemed unbearable. Elinor couldn't talk for days. Rob, characteristically, blamed himself for not calling the doctor sooner. He blamed himself for his son's death. Elinor's sorrow was so great that Rob could not penetrate it. "Home Burial," written sometime later, paints a picture of what effect this may have had on their relationship with one another. The anguish of one may not have been completely understood by the other:

> . . . .
> *He said twice over before he knew himself:*
> *"Can't a man speak of his own child he's lost?"*
>
> *"Not you! Oh, where's my hat? Oh, I don't need it!*
> *I must get out of here. I must get air.—*
> *I don't know rightly whether any man can."*
> . . . .
> *Let me into your grief. I'm not so much*
> *Unlike other folks as your standing there*
> *Apart would make me out. Give me my chance.*

Looking back on the situation, he was later able to understand the feelings of the mother, to know the anguish and rebellion of her heart that would make her cry out:

> . . . .
> *But the world's evil. I won't have grief so*
> *If I can change it. Oh, I won't, I won't!"*

Rather than being able to draw strength from each other, they were pulled apart. All Rob's old ailments—the pains in his chest and in his stomach, the nightmares, the heavy sweating—all returned anew. They were further complicated by a worsening of a hay fever condition, and he found himself exhausted from choking, coughing, sneezing, and crying.

And through all this, Belle Frost was growing steadily weaker. Finally, Rob was forced to enter her as a patient in a sanitorium in Penacook, New Hampshire. Jeanie, who was working in Boston, upbraided Rob for this. She visited her mother frequently and felt that Rob was simply trying to get rid of her. He, in turn, could not make Jeanie see that he could not manage otherwise.

To further complicate matters, the Frosts' landlady decided she had had enough of chickens and no rent and asked them to move. The world seemed to be tumbling in on them.

Elinor's mother, seeing all this and wanting desperately to help in some way, found a farm for sale on the road to Derry. She thought it might be just the place for Rob and Elinor to try to make a fresh start. She suggested to them that they ride out one day and look at it. The Magoon Place, as it was called, was a thirty-acre farm on what was called then the Londonderry Road—the road from Salem to Derry, New Hampshire. The property contained a relatively new house and barn. It had previously been a nursery, and so boasted many different varieties of fruit trees.

Elinor and Rob loved it on sight. Elinor, saying nothing to Rob, swallowed her pride, held her fine Puritan head high, and went, alone, to Grandfather Frost to ask for help. The old gentleman did not fail her. He agreed to buy the farm for them.

Rob, though, reacted strangely. Overwhelmed by all he had suffered both physically and emotionally in the last few months, he more than ever resented his need to depend on his grandfather. So instead of being grateful for the old man's generosity and concern, he interpreted it as a means of saying, Go on out and die. Good riddance to you. You've been nothing except a bother to me for years, and you're not worth anything except as a disappointment.

Rob was not even able to fully enjoy the move to Derry. The serene country setting, the orchard, fields, pasture, woodlands, and the spring that fed the little brook, all should have contributed to a feeling of peace. But they did not. Elinor was too busy getting meals, washing dishes, and caring for the baby to bother about hanging

The Derry farmhouse today. Many of Rob's best poems were written here. *Courtesy Lawrence H. Bober.*

curtains, putting rugs on the floor, or arranging furniture in the living room. Or perhaps she just didn't care.

A month after they had moved to the farm, Belle Frost died quietly at the sanitorium. She was fifty-six years old. None of her friends or relatives were with her. Her Swedenborgian pastor, John Hayes, conducted the funeral service. She was buried in Lawrence, between the graves of her husband and her grandson Elliott.

Rob was wracked with feelings of guilt—he should have kept her school going for her, he could have done more for her, he should have visited her more frequently in her last weeks. He was physically exhausted, and he had used all the cash his grandfather had given him for the move to Derry. He had sunk to the depths of despair. He even thought once again of suicide. His poem "Despair," written at this time, vividly reflects his feelings. The poem was never published.

This mood of despair and bewilderment continued through the winter, but somehow, with the coming of spring and the warm April sunlight, it began to slip away quietly, almost unnoticed.

Elinor watched as the pasture spring was cleaned. Rob took Lesley on his shoulders to show her the budding leaves and flowers. Slowly he began to assume his responsibilities. His anger, his resentment, his feeling of hopelessness were disappearing. He had "chosen life."

The Pasture

I'm going out to clean the pasture spring;
I'll only stop to rake the leaves away
(And wait to watch the water clear, I may):
I shan't be gone long.—You come too.

I'm going out to fetch the little calf
That's standing by the mother. It's so young
It totters when she licks it with her tongue.
I shan't be gone long.—You come too.

°7°

You come too

And so began the pattern of farming, teaching, and writing poetry that was to continue for the rest of his life. The rolling hills and winding roads made them both happy. The house, a simple, two-story New England farmhouse of white clapboard, had a bay window in front, a side porch, and an ell that extended back to the barn. A quarter mile back were the woods and the path to Hyla Brook.

The Frost family often picnicked and hunted for wildflowers at Hyla Brook, in the woods behind the Derry house. *Courtesy Lawrence H. Bober.*

The house had three bedrooms upstairs. Downstairs, in addition to the usual parlor, dining room, and kitchen, was a little room that had in it a bed, a sewing machine, and a sewing rocker (it had no arms). Here Elinor could mend and tend a sick child. And there was often a sick child.

In a few years the house was filled with children. On May 27, 1902, a son, Carol, was born. Just a year later, on June 27, 1903, Irma arrived. Then, on March 29, 1905, Marjorie, who was to give her father perhaps his greatest joy and his greatest sorrow, was born.

As the children were growing up, Rob spent much time with them. They were not sent to school until they were ten years old. They lived too far from town. But their father taught them to read and write. When he farmed, they trailed after him. They watched him "botanize." Then, at the dinner table, they all discussed the day's adventures:

> *"You ought to have seen what I saw on my way*
> *To the village, through Patterson's pasture today:*
> *Blueberries as big as the end of your thumb,*
> *Real sky-blue, and heavy, and ready to drum*
> *In the cavernous pail of the first one to come!*
> *And all ripe together, not some of them green*
> *And some of them ripe! You ought to have seen!"*

Studying was called "Play Time," and play school took place at 10 A.M. every day. Elinor was the teacher then. She taught them to read, to count, to sing, and to tell stories. The education they received from Rob and Elinor may well have been better than the education they would have received in school.

Lesley was typing at the age of three, spelling phonetically. She was reading at four, composing essays at five, and writing literary criticism at the age of eight. At ten she entered seventh grade.

She tells us that "Evening Time" for the children meant a short walk after supper with Papa "to see the sun go down, and hear the birds go to sleep and smell the soft mist rising from the meadow along Hyla Brook. After that we settled down in the front room for the being read aloud to that came as certainly as night followed day."

There were no assigned beds in the Derry house. The children could sleep in whichever bed they chose each night. *Courtesy Lawrence H. Bober.*

Rob and Elinor continued to read aloud to the children until they were fifteen. They read from the great works of literature that they loved themselves, passing a book back and forth between them. The children were allowed to stay and listen until they became too sleepy, however late. Often they stayed up way past their proper bedtime, listening to the two voices they loved. Sometimes they fell asleep listening. Lesley recalled this time by saying, "Our hearts were being stretched, as were our minds."

Their father felt that any book worth reading twice was worth owning. So instead of buying desserts, they bought books. Their library was really quite small, but in relation to their other possessions, it was enormous.

In their writing the children were learning to put what they saw and what they felt on paper. "If we brought Papa something born of half a look, a glance, he sent us back for a whole look. And to look meant to compare, to bring on metaphor, which is at least the cloth of poetry." Their papa was pretty good at this metaphor game himself. But the children didn't know that he was a poet.

They memorized much also. Rob told them they had to memorize in order to "know *by heart.*" They memorized all kinds of poems, among them Wordsworth's "Daffodils," Keats's "Ode on a Grecian

Urn," Henley's "Invictus," Emily Dickinson's, "There Is No Frigate Like a Book," and Coleridge's "Ancient Mariner." By the time Lesley finished one year of high school she had read and memorized whole passages of the *Iliad*. They each had their own copies of several of Shakespeare's plays—so they could act them out together.

Rob shared his delight in astronomy with his children also. He gave each child a star to "own." Lesley's was Arcturus, the brightest star in the constellation Boötes. They learned the constellations by heart too. They could recognize Orion, the Pleiades, Leo, Scorpio, Capricorn, Cassiopia, and the planets Mars, Venus, Saturn, and Jupiter. He even woke Lesley up once at midnight to show her Halley's comet.

Rob used a three-foot-long brass telescope that he had propped on a window in an upstairs bedroom. Whenever the children took turns looking through it, it brought back memories of his own boyhood, when his mother had helped him sell magazine subscriptions in order to win a telescope of his own.

The children "traveled" all over the farm with Rob and compared it to traveling to interesting places around the world. The farm became to all of them "the sweetest dream that labor knows." It became their world. They learned from it, and they loved it. They celebrated all the holidays. Once, perhaps remembering a sad Halloween many years before in San Francisco, Rob surprised the children by having jack-o'-lanterns all ready for each of them by the time it was dark. Each

LEFT: Robert Frost raking hay on the Derry farm, 1908. The children took turns riding with "Papa." *Courtesy Robin Hudnut.*

RIGHT: Rob loved to watch the children run free on the Derry farm. *Courtesy Robin Hudnut.*

pumpkin had a candle burning inside it. Then Rob hid them, each in a different place. Tiny Marjorie was allowed to go, all alone, to look for hers first. Each lantern looked different. One looked like a ghost, another had pointed paper ears glued on to make it look like an elf.

The children took turns riding beside "Papa" on the high, narrow seat of the horse-drawn hayrake. They rode beside "Mama" and held the reins of their horse, Eunice, when they went to do the Saturday night grocery shopping in Derry Depot.

Sunday usually meant an all-day picnic across the orchard to the alders. Rob cleared the underbrush with an ax and clippers and Elinor would sit on a board bench that Rob had nailed between two young pine trees. She would mend stockings or read aloud to the children, and they, in turn, would build dams, play house, using plantain leaves as their dishes, or hunt for mayflowers.

Those days—precious to all of them—were the days when Rob's poetry was growing inside him. Robert Frost was almost the perfect example of William Wordsworth's philosophy that poetry "takes its origin from emotion recollected in tranquility." Frost's memories of this life on the Derry farm were later to be transformed into some of his most beautiful poems.

In the evenings, after Elinor and the children were all asleep, Rob continued to scratch out his poems by lamplight. When he wrote "The Pasture," a poem that urges "I shan't be gone long.—You come too," he told Lesley he had written it for her, because she was the one who loved to trail after him on the farm. When she grew older, he confessed that he had actually written it for Elinor. Then, when Lesley had daughters of her own, he told them he had written it for them. Whatever "The Pasture" may have meant to the children, it is, unmistakably, a love poem to Elinor.

Rob told a friend that all the poetry was for Elinor, for a woman whose mind was "better than his own." A poem, complete and final, was his intimate gift to her. Her greatest joy was to read these gifts, but she would not let pass anything but perfection. Rob strove for this, and often held on to a poem for a long time until he knew it was right.

The center of their Derry home was Elinor, "the presence within which all else moved." "She *was* home," Lesley has said. "Going home from anywhere, at any time of day or night, meant returning to her."

The children brought her "bokas" of flowers and stories of their adventures of the day with Papa. They loved to tag along with Rob on his walks to find "old-fashioned" flowers, and then help him transplant these to their own front yard. They learned the names of all the flowers by heart, and the names of all the birds. They were part of everything their parents did.

Life was simple, even isolated. For their first eight years on the farm Rob was not away from home once after eight in the evening, and they were never invited out for a single meal. The cupboard was often bare, but life was filled to the brim, "and even above the brim." Rob Frost was finding on the Derry farm all he had come to seek.

He was going toward a way of life he believed, instinctively, to be his: toward true, old-fashioned values that ran counter to the competitive spirit, the striving for success, that were typical of the time. He and Elinor were building a world of their own beyond the reach of mill-town blight and the interference of prying relatives. While they lived for the most part in poverty, theirs was a rural poverty, not the desperate poverty of the cities. They were surrounded by natural beauty.

The farmer in him knew he had to keep the poet going. He learned to milk the cow at noon and midnight. Then, when other farmers were sleeping in order to be able to rise early for their chores, Rob could stay awake to read Shakespeare, or Virgil's *Eclogues*, or to write in the hush of a sleeping household. The warm glow of the kerosene lamp in the kitchen window soon became a familiar sight to any who chanced to walk by late at night.

His outgoing love for his children and the joy he found in the responsibilities of fatherhood were perhaps the most important elements in his recovery.

He was learning also, from his neighbors, the farmer's attitude toward the reality of life, and he was discovering new themes for his poetry. He loved to talk, and he loved to listen. He enjoyed the "actuality of gossip," he explained it. And when he met a fellow poultry farmer named John Hall, he began to listen even more carefully to his new friend's speech. He heard words that had the ring of pure poetry, and inflections of speech that captured meanings even better than words did.

Soon he began to realize that the talking tones of voice of his farmer neighbors could be an important part of form in his poetry. He was beginning to understand what Thoreau and Emerson had meant. Thoreau had written: "A true account of the actual is the purest poetry." Emerson, even before, had said:

> There is no fact in nature which does not carry the whole sense of nature. . . . The poet is he who can articulate it [the world]. . . . So the poet's habit of living should be set on a key so low that the common influences should delight him.

Now, when his French-Canadian farmer-neighbor Napoleon Guy, whose property bordered on Frost's, told him, "Good fences make good neighbors," Rob could refer to the stone wall separating the two and reply:

> *My apple trees will never get across*
> *And eat the cones under his pines, I tell him.*

The idealism of their chosen way of life on the Derry farm, and the courage that it took to achieve it, were the source of some of the most beautiful and moving poems of his early work.

But there were moments of depression, too. When there were nothing but potatoes in the cellar; when having failed to sell a batch of eggs, he returned from town in a driving snowstorm without the money he had hoped to earn to buy Christmas presents for his children; when the few poems he had sent out for publication were returned with "Rejected" stamped in red across the poem itself, then all his anguish welled up inside him and he found himself in a mood of dejection and despair, certain that he was a failure as a father, as a husband, as a poet, as a man.

The Tuft of Flowers

I went to turn the grass once after one
Who mowed it in the dew before the sun.

The dew was gone that made his blade so keen
Before I came to view the leveled scene.

I looked for him behind an isle of trees;
I listened for his whetstone on the breeze.

But he had gone his way, the grass all mown,
And I must be, as he had been—alone,

"As all must be," I said within my heart,
"Whether they work together or apart."

But as I said it, swift there passed me by
On noiseless wing a bewildered butterfly,

Seeking with memories grown dim o'er night
Some resting flower of yesterday's delight.

And once I marked his flight go round and round,
As where some flower lay withering on the ground.

And then he flew as far as eye could see,
And then on tremulous wing came back to me.

I thought of questions that have no reply,
And would have turned to toss the grass to dry;

But he turned first, and led my eye to look
At a tall tuft of flowers beside a brook,

A leaping tongue of bloom the scythe had spared
Beside a reedy brook the scythe had bared.

The mower in the dew had loved them thus,
By leaving them to flourish, not for us,

Nor yet to draw one thought of ours to him,
But from sheer morning gladness at the brim.

The butterfly and I had lit upon,
Nevertheless, a message from the dawn,

That made me hear the wakening birds around,
And hear his long scythe whispering to the ground,

And feel a spirit kindred to my own;
So that henceforth I worked no more alone;

But glad with him, I worked as with his aid,
And weary, sought at noon with him the shade;

And dreaming, as it were, held brotherly speech
With one whose thought I had not hoped to reach.

"Men work together," I told him from the heart,
"Whether they work together or apart."

· 8 ·

"Men work together," I told him from the heart

In the summer of 1901, less than a year after they had first moved to Derry, Grandfather Frost died suddenly. His will gave Rob reason to doubt his original opinion of the old man. William Frost left "To my grandson Robert Lee Frost: All silverware marked 'F,' one teaspoon marked 'Willie,' two tablespoons marked 'J. Colcord,' one napkin ring marked 'Will,' and my gold watch and chain."

The will also gave to Rob the free use and occupancy of the Derry farm for ten years and, after that, full ownership of it. In addition, it gave him an annuity (allowance) of five hundred dollars a year for ten years, then eight hundred dollars a year for the remainder of his life. Grandfather Frost had seen to it that Rob would have to stay on the farm for ten years.

But by 1906, even the annuity was not enough to pay the butcher bills for a family of six. When the local butcher asked for Rob's horse in payment of a long-overdue bill, Rob, embarrassed and ashamed, dumped the meat on the counter and stormed out of the store. He knew now that he would have to do something.

That evening, he and Elinor, in one of their frequent casual conversations around the stove in the kitchen, discussed the possibility of his returning to teaching, and the next day Rob went to Lawrence, thinking he might apply for a job there. Instead, as he was walking along Essex Street, he happened to meet William Wolcott, pastor of the First Congregationalist Church and an old friend of William Hayes Ward, editor of the *Independent*. The minister recommended that Rob apply to Pinkerton Academy, a fine, old Congregational academy in Derry. The minister there, Charles Loveland Merriam, was a friend of his, and a trustee of Pinkerton Academy. Reverend Wolcott would be happy to write to him about Frost.

When Rob finally mustered enough nerve to visit the pastor, he found him friendly and encouraging. Reverend Merriam asked if Mr. Frost would be willing to read a few of his poems before the men's league of the Congregational Church. Rob cringed. Never in his life had he read any of his own poems before an audience. Mr. Merriam countered by offering to read one for him. A few days later Rob sent to Mr. Merriam a poem he had submitted for English-A at Harvard, "The Tuft of Flowers."

On the evening of the meeting, Rob would have preferred to hide as Merriam read, but the moving rendition of the poem, ending with the lines:

> *"Men work together," I told him from the heart,*
> *"Whether they work together or apart"*

seems to have made the listeners aware that here, in this dreamy, aloof, sometime-farmer, was someone who might just have the stuff of an English teacher. As Rob walked the two miles to home that evening, he was almost afraid to think that soon he might be earning a regular salary for the first time in the ten years of his marriage.

In an exaggeration years later Rob was to say of "A Tuft of Flowers," "I wrote that poem to get my job in Pinkerton as Little Tommy Tucker sang for his supper."

Robert Frost did begin to teach at Pinkerton in the spring of 1906. He taught English literature to the sophomores. There were two sections of sophomores, and they met for an hour each, five days a week. He was paid on the basis of two-sevenths of each day's normal seven-hour teaching load of $1000 per year, approximately $285.

So evolved a pattern that was to continue for the rest of his days. He lived in two worlds—the world of the teacher, and the world of the poet-farmer.

The two-mile walk from the farm to the academy every day took him north across West-Running Brook to Derry Village, and then up the hill to the large and dignified-looking red brick building.

Pinkerton Academy was old and very formal. Morning chapel attendance was required of all, and teachers were expected to take turns leading it. To Rob this seemed frightening—and unreasonable as well. He was not used to getting up so early in the morning. So he simply skipped it, and then found himself running up the high brick steps every morning—trying not to be late for his first class.

Pinkerton Academy, where Rob taught English literature from 1906 to 1911, and developed new ideas about teaching. *Courtesy Lawrence H. Bober.*

His approach to teaching was very different from that of his colleagues, and there was some hostility toward him when he first arrived. To the faculty Frost represented new things. He defied tradition. He arrived after chapel every morning, he had no college degree, he dressed informally, and at thirty-two he was younger than most of them. He handled his classes in the same relaxed and informal manner, departing from traditional Pinkerton teaching methods.

His classes were "easy," but he covered much material. He cultivated any feeling for literature, and nursed along any talent for writing that was displayed by a student. He showed them that what makes a story of a story is "the turn, the twist, the wiggle, at least." He read to his classes regularly, often from *The Golden Treasury*. He became faculty adviser to the student publication, *Critic*, but he allowed the students to run it themselves. He believed strongly in a "hands-off" policy.

He coached several plays, including Marlowe's *Dr. Faustus*, Milton's *Comus*, and Yeats's *The Land of Heart's Desire*. Plays such as these were new at Pinkerton. They had done only Shakespeare before. Rehearsals were great fun for all involved and brought Frost and the students closer together. He had a great interest in all his students, and wanted to know all about them and their problems. This feeling for his students was communicated to them, and they, in turn, appreciated this and respected him. Any boy felt proud to be commended by Mr. Frost.

But when a parent wanted to know if her son were reading the books required for entrance to a particular college, Rob responded that the boy had better find out. He was concerned with the boy's learning to read, not with requirements. If the boy learned to read, he could then read by himself any required books or authors.

John Bartlett, one of his students then—and later a close friend—has told of an incident when Frost stood near him on the field where a few boys were passing a football back and forth. Frost asked John some questions about Devil's Den in the Pawtuckaway Mountains, about which John had written in class. He seemed, in those few minutes, to show "several hundred times" the interest in John that other teachers had. "I can still see Frost and the fall mud and the football bucking machine and the boys on that afternoon," John said years later.

The boys all enjoyed spending time with Frost outside of school. John Bartlett remembered a "walk over the turnpike to Manchester, twelve miles away, in the late afternoon, an hour spent in a bookstore, an oyster stew, and then a ride home on the electric railway."

Conversations on such walks covered many topics. Only rarely did they talk about books. Mostly Frost told stories of his early life, or they discussed school affairs, farm life in New Hampshire, current news, anything of interest at the moment. If, as they walked, they passed a farmhouse and the aroma of freshly fried doughnuts came out to them, Frost might propose that they stop and buy some. If he saw a fern he had not seen since he was last in the Lake Willoughby region, he would point it out. If it got dark, Frost would take the opportunity to start the boy's astronomical education and take five minutes to study the heavens.

Rob's concern for and understanding of the young, both his own and those he taught, was evidenced in many ways. He watched, at Pinkerton, as John Bartlett and a young girl named Margaret Abbott, from Derry Depot, slowly fell in love with one another. Perhaps the situation, so reminiscent of his own early courtship of Elinor, prompted him to interfere.

When he watched Margaret decide that she was too young to be so in love with John, and then saw John's misery as Margaret avoided him, he decided he had to act. Taking Margaret aside, he told her, "Go talk to John! He's miserable." She needed nothing more to erase her doubts. She went to him, and never again questioned the rightness of her love for him.

John Bartlett was to say years later, referring to other incidents as well, "That was what friendship meant to Rob Frost, help to the maximum when a boy needed it."

As a teacher in the classroom, Rob encouraged the boys and girls to write out of their everyday experiences. He suggested that they describe whatever they saw fun or beauty in, but never found in books. "Good writing," he said, "grows out of having something to say. Write out of your own observations, experiences, insights."

He wrote on the blackboard at Pinkerton:

> uncommon in experience—uncommon in writing
> common in experience—common in writing
> uncommon in experience—common in writing
> common in experience—uncommon in writing

The last, he told his students, was the kind of material to search for. This became a famous formula for the boys and girls.

He refused to ask questions of his students that he could answer himself. He wanted them to seek what *he* wanted most—"the freedom of my materials."

A story is told about an incident that occurred at Pinkerton. It tells much about the man. Frost had asked for some written work. When he entered his classroom he found a pile of themes on his desk. His native "orneriness" took over.

"Anything here anyone wants to keep?"
They shook their heads no. So I asked them again
and they said no again.
"All right. If you don't value them enough to keep
them, I don't value them enough to want to read them."
And I threw them all into the wastepaper basket.
"I'm no perfunctory reader of perfunctory writing."

In the spring of the following year Rob developed a nearly fatal case of pneumonia. He was still recuperating when Elinor gave birth to their fourth daughter, Elinor Bettina, on June 18, 1907. The baby lived only four days. Elinor accepted the loss with the despairing fatalism that had become part of her. Rob, once again, blamed himself.

Because he was ill, he had received no salary from Pinkerton for the spring term, so now he sent some poems to the *Independent*. None were accepted. All the money he had was the annuity check for five hundred dollars from his grandfather's trust fund, and the assurance that if he were strong enough, he could teach at Pinkerton again in the fall, for the annual salary of one thousand dollars.

As the summer wore on and he recuperated from the pneumonia, he began to be plagued by hay fever. Finally, with Elinor still quietly distraught over the loss of their baby and worried about Rob's health as well, Rob decided the whole family needed a change. He took them to a farmhouse owned by the Lynches, high up in the White Mountains. The clean, dry air was bracing and healing for Rob. The children loved the freedom of the mountain life, the pony they could ride, and mostly, the companionship of other children for the first time in their lives. And Elinor relaxed.

Rob described this summer as "one of the pleasantest we have

The Frost family at the Lynch farm in Bethlehem, New Hampshire, in the summer of 1907. Left to right: Rob, Marjorie, Lesley, Elinor, Irma, Carol. *Courtesy Robin Hudnut.*

had for years. . . . There is a pang here that makes poetry. I rather like to gloat over it.''

That Christmas, as on many others, there was no money for gifts for the children, so Rob decided to carve little wooden animals for them. He finished a pig for Carol at two o'clock on Christmas morning. But then he decided that the pig needed a pen. He started whittling again. Elinor, sitting beside him in her rocker, dozed off. When she awoke at dawn, she found that Rob had just finished the pen.

In 1909 Frost was offered the position of principal of Pinkerton Academy. He was flattered, but refused it because he feared his lack of a college degree would cause criticism of the academy. He was secretly proud though that he had been asked, and proud also that he had been permitted to draw up a new statement of the English curriculum for publication in the academy's annual catalogue.

His aim, he stated in the catalogue, was to bring his students "under the *influence* of great books, and to teach them the *satisfaction* of superior speech." Freshmen were expected to read selections from literature aloud even *before* they discussed them. Here Frost was beginning to celebrate the speaking voice, which would later become so important to him in his own poetry. The many years during which his mother had read aloud to him were reaping their reward.

Later he encouraged students in their senior year to reread selections that they "remembered with pleasure"—to enjoy them for their own sake, *"from sheer morning gladness at the brim."*

One day in the spring of 1909, a stranger quietly walked into one of Rob's classes and took a seat at the back of the room. Later that afternoon he did the same thing again. Then he remained after school to tell Frost that he was Henry Morrison, Dartmouth '95, superintendent of public instruction for the state of New Hampshire. Robert Frost's new ideas about teaching English were spreading throughout New Hampshire. Now Superintendent Morrison wanted Frost to speak on his methods of teaching at a small convention of New Hampshire teachers.

Rob planned his talk on the train trip to Exeter. He would tell them that books should be used in English classes so that students would be lonely forever afterward without books of their own. He would tell them how he caught the students' interest, and how he helped them take pride in presenting an idea well, whether orally or in writing.

But by the time he arrived in Exeter he was so frightened by the prospect of speaking to a roomful of teachers that he thought he would not be able to go through with it. In an attempt to take his mind off his worries, he put a pebble in each of his shoes, hoping the pain would distract him. It did not. But he gave his talk, and it was so well received that he was asked to repeat it several times throughout New Hampshire. He was gaining desperately needed confidence in himself.

❧

Over the years Elinor had suffered much from Rob's sensitivities, his easily hurt pride, his quick temper. Her best defense had always been her silence. But she, as no one else could, understood his fierce determination—his need—to write poetry, and his frustration at his failure to make a living at it for his family. For her then, there was great relief in seeing this slowly evolving confidence in this man she loved.

In the fall of that year (1909) the new principal took over at Pinkerton, and there began a relationship between him and Frost that

Robert Frost (without a cap) as umpire of the baseball team at Pinkerton Academy, 1911. *Courtesy Jones Library, Amherst.*

was to prove long and fruitful. The man was Ernest L. Silver, a graduate of Pinkerton Academy and of Dartmouth, and about the same age as Frost.

Both men enjoyed sports, and often appeared together on the athletic field to watch the boys—or even to toss a baseball back and forth between them. Both rejected the strict formality that had marked the academy before, and brought to it a new, relaxed atmosphere.

And Rob was writing poetry again. From the time his self-confidence had begun to improve, he found he was writing more and more. He found also, much to his amazement, that the harder he worked at Pinkerton, the greater the incentive to write poetry.

When, in the summer of 1911, Silver accepted the position of principal of the New Hampshire State Normal School in Plymouth, a school to train teachers, and asked Rob to teach there with him, Frost was hesitant about accepting. He and Elinor had long discussions about it—viewing it from all possible aspects. Finally, after much agonizing over the decision, Rob accepted the position but made it clear that he would have to be free to resign at the end of the year if he so desired.

Since there were no openings in the field of English at the school, Frost would teach psychology and the history of education. Both Morrison and Silver felt that Frost's value to the school would be so great that it didn't matter what he taught—as long as he was on the staff. His new sense of self-confidence was being reinforced. Suddenly he had the walk and the bearing of a man going someplace.

Rob stored their furniture and moved his family north to Plymouth, in the foothills of the White Mountains. And his rebellion against conformity continued.

His first act when he began to teach was to alter the curriculum: "Take them to the basement," he told the girls, referring to the old volumes of the required *History of Education.* "We won't need them. Instead we'll get a few books that have lighted teachers down the ages—Plato's *Republic,* Rousseau's *Emile,* and others." He told the girls he hoped they would like these books well enough to buy copies of them for their own shelves, to reread at leisure after they had begun teaching. By now he had established a pattern of teaching that simply put good books into the hands of his students.

As principal, Ernest Silver was given a large "cottage" in which to live. This was the traditional campus residence for the principal. Silver's wife was an invalid, and therefore was living temporarily with her parents in Portsmouth. In an act of friendship he offered to share his cottage, rent-free, with the Frosts.

But Silver was not prepared for Elinor's informality—her indifference to housework. It was far more important to her to spend time with her children than to clean a house, prepare a meal, or wash the dinner dishes. Silver's attempt to entertain visiting dignitaries proved very embarrassing to him on several occasions. When he jokingly said something about Elinor to Frost, Rob, enraged, retorted, "But she's mine!"

Lesley, Carol, Irma, and Marjorie were all of school age now, and were attending Plymouth Normal School. The campus of the school provided tennis courts for the students, so Lesley and Carol learned to play. Their father spent so much time helping them develop their skills that he became an excellent player himself.

Frost soon discovered a young English teacher, Sidney Cox, who had just graduated from college. Cox greatly admired Frost, and eventually came to look on him as a father. The two men took long walks

Marjorie (holding ball) was the mascot for the basketball team at Plymouth State Normal School. *Courtesy Robin Hudnut.*

together through the hills, back roads, and vales around Plymouth. They played tennis together, and they sat through long evenings in conversation and in reading poetry aloud. Cox described it:

> When we returned from those walks he would take me to the drugstore for a glass of white grapejuice. . . . Other times he took me home with him for a dinner of leg of lamb. When the kids had gone to bed he would read from thin, attractive volumes of poetry . . . his uniquely vibrating voice a flexible instrument for the speech music of many emotions. Tones, he said, pauses and rushes and intensities of sound are more revealing than the definition value of the words. . . . He had once recited "Lycidas," he said, all of it, alone on the summit of Mount Lafayette.

In spite of all this, Rob was restless. The poetry was gnawing at him from within. While many poems had been written, and several even published in *The Youth's Companion* and *Forum Magazine,* he still wasn't satisfied.

The poem "Reluctance," written so long ago when he had despaired that Elinor would ever marry him, had been bought by Thomas Bird Mosher, a Maine publisher and book collector, for inclusion in *Amphora,* one of Mosher's publications. Frost had great respect for Mosher, who also published a small monthly anthology of short but significant pieces of prose and poetry. It was the year 1912, Rob was thirty-eight years old, and teaching was again becoming a burden. Then in January during the relaxed interval between school terms, he composed a number of poems in a sudden feverish burst of creativity, among them his lovely song "October."

O hushed October morning mild,
Thy leaves have ripened to the fall;
Tomorrow's wind, if it be wild,
Should waste them all.
The crows above the forest call;
Tomorrow they may form and go.
O hushed October morning mild,
Begin the hours of this day slow.
Make the day seem to us less brief.
Hearts not averse to being beguiled,
Beguile us in the way you know.
Release one leaf at break of day;
At noon release another leaf;
One from our trees, one far away.
Retard the sun with gentle mist;
Enchant the land with amethyst.
Slow, slow!
For the grapes' sake, if they were all,
Whose leaves already are burnt with frost,
Whose clustered fruit must else be lost—
For the grapes' sake along the wall.

This one, he knew, was moving in the right direction. He had achieved the graceful turning of words into original combinations that he had been striving for. But he needed to be alone with his poems for a while. He "felt impelled to lose myself among strangers, to write poetry without further scandal to friends or family."

The Road Not Taken

Two roads diverged in a yellow wood,
And sorry I could not travel both
And be one traveler, long I stood
And looked down one as far as I could
To where it bent in the undergrowth;

Then took the other, as just as fair,
And having perhaps the better claim,
Because it was grassy and wanted wear;
Though as for that, the passing there
Had worn them really about the same,

And both that morning equally lay
In leaves no step had trodden black.
Oh, I kept the first for another day!
Yet knowing how way leads on to way,
I doubted if I should ever come back.

I shall be telling this with a sigh
Somewhere ages and ages hence:
Two roads diverged in a wood, and I—
I took the one less traveled by,
And that has made all the difference.

∘ 9 ∘

I took the one less traveled by

For several weeks the children had been hearing their mother and father talk about leaving Derry, about going someplace where it wouldn't matter if they were poor, and Papa could write poetry. They had heard John and Margaret Bartlett's letters read aloud, begging them to visit them on Vancouver Island, British Columbia, the largest island off the west coast of North America. They knew that John and Margaret had been students of their father at Pinkerton Academy, and that they had married and gone to Vancouver to live. But their mother seemed to prefer England. "Let's go to England and live under thatch," they heard her say.

They were all gathered around the stove in the kitchen, keeping Elinor company as she ironed, when the subject came up again. As they debated between Canada and England, their father opted to join the Bartletts in the wild, natural beauty of Vancouver, with its mountains to climb and its beaches to walk. Suddenly, though, he suggested they toss a coin. He took a nickel out of his pocket, said, "Heads, England, tails, Vancouver." It was heads. The coin had chosen England. And in that moment, their future was decided.

They spent the summer in eager anticipation, contemplating fresh scenery, the peace for Rob to be able to write, and the excitement of change. In England, they thought, Rob could have time for writing poetry away from the burdens of teaching. So they started in earnest to try to sell the farm.

The six Frosts on a picnic before sailing for England, 1911. At left, Rob, Elinor. At right, front to back: Marjorie, Irma, Carol, Lesley. *Courtesy Robin Hudnut.*

Toward the end of August, Frost asked Silver to help his family finish packing while he went ahead to Boston to buy steamship tickets. They had stored their furniture, planning to take with them bedclothes, two floor rugs, books, and some pictures. The only furniture they took were two chairs, a rocking chair for Elinor and a favorite leather-upholstered Morris chair for Robert to write in. On Friday, August 23, 1912, Silver put Elinor and the children on the train for Boston. When they arrived there, they went directly to the pier, where Rob was waiting for them.

Shortly before 5:00 A.M. on Saturday, August 24, the British ship SS *Parisian* left Boston Harbor bound for Glasgow, Scotland. On board were 211 barrels of apples, 46,665 bushels of wheat, and a full list of passengers, among them Robert and Elinor Frost and their four children, Lesley, thirteen; Carol, ten; Irma, nine; and Marjorie, seven.

Like his father before him, Robert Frost had decided to break away from the life he had known. William Frost had traveled across a continent to seek his fortune. Now, almost forty years later, his son was leaving the home of his ancestors and traveling across the ocean.

Robert Frost was already older than his father had been when he died, had no college degree, knew not one person in England, and had no letters of introduction. Still he felt compelled to leave a job where he was respected and that earned him $1100 per year, and uproot his wife and children in order to write his poetry.

He had $1100 from the sale of the Derry farm, $800 a year from his grandfather's estate, and that was all. But he had made his decision and they were off.

> *I shall be telling this with a sigh*
> *Somewhere ages and ages hence:*
> *Two roads diverged in a wood, and I—*
> *I took the one less traveled by,*
> *And that has made all the difference.*

Rob, Elinor, and Lesley were seasick for the first few days, but the other children suffered only a few hours of discomfort. On the whole, the trip was an exciting adventure for all of them. Several times, though, Rob, standing at the rail by himself and looking out at the vast expanse of water all around him, thought back to a phrase that he had said to himself the week before when he was saying goodbye to Superintendent Silver in Plymouth, "Quit you like men." This admonition, from Paul's first Epistle to the Corinthians, seems to have given him the strength he needed.

They arrived in Glasgow on the morning of September 3, and left there immediately by train for London. They traveled all day across Scotland and then down through England, arriving in London about seven o'clock at night. From the station, Frost telephoned to reserve rooms at the Premier Hotel, a small annex to the more stately Imperial House. Then he bundled his weary family into a taxicab for the exciting trip across London to the hotel in Russell Square.

But it didn't take Rob and Elinor long to recoup their strength. A bath, a change of clothes, a little supper, and they were off. Lesley was asked to remain at the hotel to look after the younger children while their parents celebrated their arrival in London by attending a performance of George Bernard Shaw's *Fanny's First Play*.

Although they were all alone in London, the largest city in the world, they didn't feel alone. For the next week they followed a pattern. During the day, while Robert looked for a house for them in the nearby suburbs, Elinor took the children sight-seeing in London. This was the time of the reign of King George V, grandfather of the present Queen Elizabeth of England. London, the capital of England and the chief city of the entire British Commonwealth of nations, was then one of the most important and exciting cities in the world.

Each day Elinor and the children would set out early in the morning to see some part of London. They walked along the banks of the river Thames, watching some of the hundreds of ships that left the port of London each month for harbors all around the world.

As they walked they saw London's spires, domes, and palaces rising gracefully from the water. They saw the supremely beautiful Westminster Abbey, where British monarchs are crowned in wonderful, colorful ceremonies. They saw Buckingham Palace, where the king lived, and were particularly excited by the guardsmen there in their bright red uniforms and great bearskin hats. They rode in a boat down the Thames River to the Tower of London, the oldest monument in the city, its chilling gray stone walls evoking the history of England.

Perhaps, though, they liked best the chance to meet back at the hotel at teatime, and to share the excitement of their adventures with Papa. As they told him one day of their walk through Charing Cross, then as now the book center of the world, Robert was delighted to hear their descriptions of the arrays of books in old bookstalls, and of the print shops. They even tried to describe for him the special smell of the books.

❧

Elinor loved these days with the children, sharing the excitement of discovery with them, and reliving the history of England. She found London "splendid." But she liked even more the evenings. Then she and Rob, alone together, would wander through Covent Garden with its bustling flower and vegetable market and go to a play at the Drury Lane Theatre or, perhaps, see the Sadlers Wells with its "singers, clowns, conjurers, posture makers, harlequins." Drama was important in London.

While Elinor and the children were exploring London, Rob was busy trying to locate a suitable place for them to live. They knew they wanted to live in the country. They hoped to be able to grow vegetables in order to save some money and, in this way, to be able to prolong their stay in England. Rob recalled that he had read a column entitled "Country Walks" in the English newspaper *T.P.'s Weekly* that indicated that its author was familiar with the rural areas near London. Visiting the columnist at the newspaper office one day, Frost found him to be a friendly, pipe-smoking ex-policeman, happy to share his knowledge and act as guide.

Now, with his newfound friend, Rob would set out each day for another little town near London, looking for just the right cottage. One day, shortly after they had begun the search, they took the new line of the Great Western Railway from Paddington Station going west and got off at Beaconsfield, in Buckinghamshire, twenty-one miles from London. Perhaps it was the name of the real estate agent of the town, plainly visible from the Beaconsfield railway station, that prompted him to get off there, but Mr. A. C. Frost, agent, very quickly rented to Mr. Robert Frost a tiny bungalow on the edge of the countryside.

"The Bungalow," as it was called, was one of three small houses on Reynolds Road, set behind high hedges of laurel and red osier dogwood. It was not far from the middle of the village. Tiny, but close to both London and rural life, it offered to all the Frosts exactly what they were looking for. Set in the leafy Buckinghamshire countryside, the softly sloping Chiltern Hills to the north and, on a clear night, the lights of London barely visible in the distance to the west, it was ideal.

They purchased enough furniture to get along with for $125, planning to sell it when they were ready to leave. Then, on September 13, 1912, they moved from the Premier Hotel in London to the Bungalow in Beaconsfield.

When they got off the train at Beaconsfield, they walked up the road to the cottage, Rob and Irma stopping along the way at the grocer's and the baker's. Soon they saw, just ahead, some men moving furniture into a low, vine-covered stucco cottage with a large, grassy lawn in front. Elinor and three of the children ran ahead, then waited for Rob and Irma to come and unlock the side door. As they walked in Rob put the key on a nail just inside the door, then walked through the house, showing Irma the three bedrooms, the living room with its fireplace, and the kitchen. When Irma wrote in her journal that night, she said there were some men washing the kitchen when they arrived because it was awfully dirty.

The others had already gone through the house and were outside in the garden, so Rob and Irma followed. Here there were a greenhouse, a summer house, and a pretty garden with pear trees, strawberry beds, and lots of flowers. It was deeply hedged in, English style, and its privacy afforded them an extra room.

Ultimately, neighbors were to marvel at how the six Frosts could fit into such limited space, but the cottage never seemed cramped to them. They immediately—as was their custom—made the kitchen into a living room where they all congregated around the stove and talked, keeping Elinor company as she cooked, ironed, or sewed. She, fragile though she was, took on British housekeeping with no complaint. She accepted the fact that the brick stoves, while picturesque, were hard to heat.

In the evenings she would draw her rocking chair, brought from home, close to the fireplace and darn while she worried about colds, pneumonia, and poetry. Rob often sat opposite her in his own Derry Morris chair. He later described this by saying, "The chair I could write in had to have just the right arms to support a shelf stolen from the closet and not to interfere with my elbows."

The family quickly settled into a happy and peaceful life. As he had back in Derry, Rob spent much time exploring the countryside—taking the children on long walks down country roads and constantly comparing the landscape to the New Hampshire scenes they had left behind.

After visiting elementary schools in the neighborhood, Rob and Elinor decided to keep the children at home. Elinor was fearful that if she sent them to one of the free county council schools, they would go back to America speaking cockney English. A good private school was out of the question. They could not afford it. In a letter to their friend Sidney Cox, Elinor told him that one school would influence the children to look down on a certain part of humanity, while the other would influence them to look up to a particular class of people. Neither was acceptable to her. Therefore, she had decided, she would teach them herself. The children did not complain.

Rob and Elinor continued their teaching philosophy of the Derry days by encouraging the children to keep a journal. Here, in Beaconsfield, it took the form of a literary game. The children did little stories, poems, watercolors, and drawings, put these on folded type-writer paper, and bound them in heavy paper covers. They called their venture *The Bouquet,* and elected Lesley editor-in-chief. The greenhouse was converted into their publishing house, and there Lesley typed the contributions on the little typewriter they had brought with them from Derry.

Rob, though enjoying England, his closeness with his family, his complete freedom to roam, to write, to botanize, to share with his children his love for astronomy, still found that he missed what he had left behind. Alone one night, sitting on the floor by the fireplace long after the others had gone to sleep, he pulled out a sheaf of poems he had brought with him and started to read through them. He spread them out on the floor in the lamplight and started to burn what he felt he could spare. These were the poems he had written between 1892 and 1912—the poems of youth. Many had been written on the Derry farm.

He began to look for a pattern in the ones he saved—a unifying element—a way to arrange them. As he thought about them he became more and more excited, realizing finally that the poems did represent the thoughts of a young man who had struggled hard to find his own direction. They were, in reality, the story of his own life, " . . . the unforced expression of a life I was forced to live." He saw that the early ones were written at a time when he thought he preferred nature to people, when he had been unhappy and at the mercy of himself. Then, slowly, in a sort of "clinical curve," they began to swing back toward people.

He put the unburned poems in his pocket and went to bed. The next day he suddenly realized that there was enough of a unity in the poems so that they might be woven into a book. He thought of Longfellow's words

> *A boy's will is the wind's will*
> *And the thoughts of youth are long, long thoughts*

and he had his title: *A Boy's Will.*

Excited, he prevailed upon Lesley to type them on their little Blickensderfer typewriter, then took the manuscript to his only friend in London, the columnist on *T.P.'s Weekly.* That man informed Frost a little book like that might cost him about fifteen pounds to have published. Frost was taken aback. He would never publish a book at his own expense, he told his friend. After a while, the policeman-turned-columnist suggested David Nutt, a small publishing firm that he knew handled some poetry. Rob, remembering that he had seen some verse by William Ernest Henley under this imprint, felt that it might be the place.

Rob found the Nutt office at 6 Bloomsbury Street, went in, and told them he had some poems and would like to see David Nutt. A strange, sad lady, dressed all in black, emerged, saying in a French accent, "I will speak for David Nutt."

Rob had no way of knowing that David Nutt was dead. He simply left the manuscript with her, with great misgivings, although she promised to let him know her decision within a few days. She kept her word. Less than a week later, in a letter dated October 26, 1912, Robert Frost learned that his first book had been accepted for publication. It was less than two months since they had arrived in England.

> She never told me anything, though—the relict.
> Whether she admired the book, or why, or who advised
> her to admire and publish. To have nobody in England
> to advise or confer with was baffling.

But he had won his gamble. The entire course of his life and career had been changed in the tiny, country cottage in Beaconsfield. His dream of almost twenty years—from the time he had first sent poems to Susan Hayes Ward "with a view to a volume someday"— had finally been realized. The genius that had been bottled up within him for forty years was about to be recognized.

Mrs. Nutt, who was actually Mrs. Alfred Nutt, widow of the

son of David Nutt and manager of David Nutt and Company, gave Frost a contract promising him 12.5 percent of the royalties from the sale of the book. But she did not give him an advance payment on them. Nor would she pay any royalty on the first 250 copies of the book. And even more painful, Rob was obligated to offer to David Nutt and Company his next four books on the same terms. But a volume of his poems would be published, and he was glad.

With Christmas just two months away and money very tight, the children once again, as they had done in Derry, found themselves bargaining with the grocer for some of the old wood he kept stored in his back room. Three or four pennies worth per child would provide enough wood to make each other presents.

It was a hard winter for all of them, and a lonely one, but with their extra American pennies they were able to buy the eggs, milk, and meat that some of their English neighbors couldn't afford. And Rob was comforted by the knowledge that he would soon see his book in print.

Mending Wall

Something there is that doesn't love a wall,
That sends the frozen-ground-swell under it
And spills the upper boulders in the sun,
And makes gaps even two can pass abreast.
The work of hunters is another thing:
I have come after them and made repair
Where they have left not one stone on a stone,
But they would have the rabbit out of hiding,
To please the yelping dogs. The gaps I mean,
No one has seen them made or heard them made,
But at spring mending-time we find them there.
I let my neighbor know beyond the hill;
And on a day we meet to walk the line
And set the wall between us once again.
We keep the wall between us as we go.
To each the boulders that have fallen to each.
And some are loaves and some so nearly balls
We have to use a spell to make them balance:
"Stay where you are until our backs are turned!"
We wear our fingers rough with handling them.
Oh, just another kind of outdoor game,
One on a side. It comes to little more:
There where it is we do not need the wall:

He is all pine and I am apple orchard.
My apple trees will never get across
And eat the cones under his pines, I tell him.
He only says, "Good fences make good neighbors."
Spring is the mischief in me, and I wonder
If I could put a notion in his head:
"*Why* do they make good neighbors? Isn't it
Where there are cows? But here there are no cows.
Before I built a wall I'd ask to know
What I was walling in or walling out,
And to whom I was like to give offense.
Something there is that doesn't love a wall,
That wants it down." I could say "Elves" to him,
But it's not elves exactly, and I'd rather
He said it for himself. I see him there,
Bringing a stone grasped firmly by the top
In each hand, like an old-stone savage armed.
He moves in darkness as it seems to me,
Not of woods only and the shade of trees.
He will not go behind his father's saying,
And he likes having thought of it so well
He says again, "Good fences make good neighbors."

· 10 ·

Something there is that doesn't love a wall

J ust one month after his book had been accepted for publication, Rob noticed an announcement in the November issue of *Poetry Review*. It told of the opening of a "Bookshop for the sale of poetry, and of all books, pamphlets and periodicals connected directly or indirectly with poetry" at 35 Devonshire Street, Theobalds Road, by Harold Monro, a Scotsman who was a Cambridge graduate, a poet, and the editor of the *Poetry Review*.

Monro, Frost soon learned, was associated with a group of poets who called themselves the Georgian Poets, taking their name from the coronation of George V in 1911. The group included Rupert Brooke, Walter de la Mare, Wilfred Gibson, John Drinkwater, and Lascelles Abercrombie. Its leader then was Edward Marsh, a Cambridge graduate. Frost liked the Georgians because they, too, had discarded the nineteenth-century style and made poetry of common life. Like Frost, they used the language of everyday speech. He decided to attend the opening. Rob probably looked forward also to an opportunity to meet and share ideas with other poets. For many years now, he had had no contact with any creative minds to match his own—no opportunity for the give-and-take so essential for any artist.

On January 8,1913, Frost made his way to 35 Devonshire Street. But the eighteenth-century house that held the bookshop, as well as the offices of the *Poetry Review,* was so crowded that he had to sit on a staircase leading to a balcony. Here he found himself sitting next to

"My life was a risk I had to take, and took." The first formal photograph of Robert Frost as a poet, taken in England, 1913. *Courtesy Dartmouth College Library.*

a young man named Frank S. Flint, a poet who had published his first volume of poems, *In the Net of Stars,* in 1909.

The two men began to talk and Flint guessed that Frost was an American by the shoes he was wearing. Before the evening had ended, Frost had bought a copy of *In the Net of Stars,* Flint had promised to review *A Boy's Will,* and had suggested that Frost try to meet Ezra Pound, an American poet living in England. Pound, although eleven years younger than Frost, was already established as a respected poet and literary leader, both in London and in America. Frost's warm letter of praise of Flint's poetry, sent to Flint the next day, transformed the acquaintance into a friendship.

Within a few weeks, the entire Frost family was aglow with the excitement of the arrival of the galley proofs of *A Boy's Will*. The galleys, long sheets of the printed version of his poems, came to Rob for corrections before the type was to be set onto the pages. Then, a short time later, actual page proofs arrived for correction before the final printing. A set of these page proofs, stamped "First Revise, 30 Jan. 1913" was given to him to keep. In a burst of pride, Rob sent these to John Bartlett in Vancouver.

In the meantime, Frank Flint had kept his promise to Frost and had prevailed upon Ezra Pound to invite the American poet to call on him. This Pound did, sending Frost a calling card bearing his address, beneath which he had written, "At home—sometimes."

Hurt by the arrogance of the message, but understanding full well the importance of meeting Ezra Pound, Frost eventually did visit him. The meeting, though, was a surprise to Frost. After climbing a dark stairway to reach the second-floor rooms in which Pound lived, Rob was startled when his knock on the door was answered by a young man with tousled red hair, vivid blue eyes, and a neatly trimmed red beard, wrapped in an ornate purple dressing gown. Frost had interrupted Pound's "bird-bath."

Pound immediately chastised Frost for having waited a month to come to call, then asked to see a copy of his book. When Frost admitted he had not yet seen one, Pound declared they would go promptly to the publisher and demand a copy. He was certain it was ready. This they did, and, when they arrived, Pound took charge, accepting the first bound copy of *A Boy's Will* himself as Frost stood by and watched. The thin little volume, bound in pebble-grained and copper-colored cloth, remained in Pound's hands. "I had to walk back to his lodgings with *him* holding *my* book," Rob complained later to Elinor.

When the two men arrived back at Pound's, Frost was instructed to keep busy by reading a magazine while Pound sat down to read the poems. At one point, Pound, chuckling at one of the poems, looked up and said, "You don't mind our liking this?"

"Oh, no, go right ahead," Frost replied.

When Pound expressed his liking for the little poem "In Neglect,"

They leave us so to the way we took,
  As two in whom they were proved mistaken,
That we sit sometimes in the wayside nook,
With mischievous, vagrant, seraphic look,
  And try *if we cannot feel forsaken*

Frost made the mistake of telling him the story behind the lines, changing it and embroidering it as he had so often done as a child. But this time he would pay a price far greater than the beatings he had received from his father.

Frost told Pound how his grandfather had mistreated him and sent him out to the Derry farm to die. He told how he had been deprived of money that should have been his by his grandfather and his uncle Elihu Colcord. He also told of the difficulty in finding a magazine editor who would publish his poems.

A little later Pound said, "I guess you'd better run along home. I'm going to review your book." This Pound did, then sent the review to Harriet Monroe, who had just begun to publish a poetry review in Chicago called *Poetry: A Magazine of Verse*. When the review appeared in the May 1913 issue it contained some of Frost's remarks about American editors and about his grandfather and uncle. Rob was horrified, and Elinor wept. It was difficult to know whether Pound would do more harm or good. A rift between the two poets was already beginning to form.

Pound did lend his copy of *A Boy's Will* to the poet William Butler Yeats, though, who declared it the best poetry written in America for a long time. Yeats then indicated that he would like to meet Frost. To Rob, who considered Yeats his favorite living poet, this was quite an honor.

Very soon thereafter, Frost and Pound went together to one of Yeats's Monday nights "at home." Pound wore his velvet jacket for the occasion. The room in which they sat and talked was darkened by heavy curtains and lit only by candles. Rob felt a little uneasy and awkward all evening and, although he did accept Yeats's invitation to come again, he was never able to establish a rapport with this man whose poetry he had for so long admired.

When *A Boy's Will* was published on April 1, 1913, the first reviews were not altogether favorable. Rob was discouraged and disappointed. Yeats, who had said privately how much he admired Frost's poetry, refused to say so publicly. Rob's disappointment brought back feelings of homesickness, and he found himself writing to Superintendent Silver back in Plymouth, "I see lots of Americans. . . . I yearn toward them. . . . I'm a Yank from Yanksville." He was now faced with the decision of what to do next.

In spite of his longings for America, he was still able to see the beauty of England. In May, as the gloom and chill of winter gave way to glorious sunshine, he wrote to his friend Sidney Cox, "We are up to our eyes in the flowers of an English spring. . . . I like that about the English—they all have time to dig in the ground for the unutilitarian flower. I mean the men. It marks the great difference between them and our men."

But his homesickness was soon to be turned into poetry. It drove his thoughts back to memories of the Derry farm. In fact, his longings for the farm now had the effect of intensifying his recollections. He never saw New England as clearly as when he was in old England. Out of these recollections came three lyrics, today among his best-loved poems. One began, "Something there is that doesn't love a wall." Another was "After Apple-Picking." The third, written while wandering around the muddy yard at the Bungalow, was "Birches." This last one he put in his pocket to bring home to America with him. The Yankee in him liked to hoard his poems. He spent money, but he kept poems in his bank, "acquiring interest."

The homesickness brought back also memories of the talk of his old New Hampshire neighbors, particularly his friend John Hall, and before long Rob knew what he would do. His next volume of poems would be a collection of dramatic narratives, written in poetic lines that sounded like talk. He would call this volume *North of Boston,* suggested by a Boston newspaper he remembered that had advertised property for sale in an area north of Boston. He would show again, as he had in *A Boy's Will,* that individuals could survive tragedy "by and with and through the strength of affirmative, outgoing love." He began to realize that the stubborn, rocky soil he had struggled with on the Derry farm for ten years had yielded not crops, but poetry.

While on a holiday in Scotland, Rob's memories of this stone wall on the Derry farm inspired "Mending Wall." *Courtesy Lawrence H. Bober.*

A poem should "begin in delight and end in wisdom . . . It begins as a lump in the throat, a sense of wrong, a homesickness, a lovesickness." Rob's handwritten draft of "Birches" with edits. *Photo by Lawrence H. Bober, courtesy Jones Library, Amherst.*

Rob continued to suffer the torture of not knowing whether he had succeeded or failed with *A Boy's Will* until he returned from a short vacation with his family in Scotland in September. In fact, it was while walking in the little village of Kingsbarns, just north of Edinburgh, where they had spent their holiday, that Rob came upon two old stone walls of the kind he had known in Derry. Still homesick for America, and "thinking of the old [boundary] wall that I hadn't mended in several years and which must be in terrible condition," he wrote the first draft of "Mending Wall."

Now he found that in the month they had been gone three new reviews of *A Boy's Will* had appeared, all favorable. Perhaps he liked best the anonymous review that began:

> It is undoubtedly the work of a true poet. . . . No one who really cares for poetry should miss this little book. We have not the slightest idea who Mr. Robert Frost may be, but we welcome him unhesitatingly to the ranks of the poets born.

But praise of the poetry always brought to him thoughts of the worst parts of himself. Rob was plagued with feelings of guilt—guilt that his best poetry was produced at the expense of those he dearly loved, his wife and his children.

The relationship between Rob and Elinor was a paradox: it was idyllic, and it was haunted. It was this strong love for one another and Elinor's unfailing support of Rob that made the poetry possible, but it took a heavy toll.

Rob knew the children were unhappy and homesick. For a brief time they had attended a school in Beaconsfield, but had complained so bitterly that Elinor had resumed teaching them. He knew that Elinor was overtaxed and ill. The strains of educating the children, and of entertaining his newly acquired friends, added to her normal house-keeping chores, were more than her fragile health could bear. Delicate, shy, seldom at ease with strangers, she was plagued with numerous illnesses, yet she never complained. As the bleak winter months wore on, Rob took over the care of the house and children. They became more and more anxious to return home.

In a letter to Silver, Frost expressed the feelings of them all when he said:

> Homesickness makes us news hungry. Every time the
> postman bangs the letter-slot-door our mouths go open
> and our eyes shut like birds in a nest and we can't move
> for a moment.

But he knew he had achieved a personal and original form. His faith in himself was strengthening, and he was able to refuse Pound's invitation to join his group of imagist poets. He knew he had to work alone. The Imagists, among them Pound and Amy Lowell, worked together, shortening one another's poetry. When Pound, to illustrate his theory, said of one of Frost's poems, "You've done it in fifty words. I've shortened it to forty-eight," Frost could reply, "And spoiled my metre, my idiom, and idea."

Soon he was working again. He began to prepare the way for *North of Boston,* circulating poems from it. He started by visiting the young poet Wilfred Wilson Gibson, taking along a few of his unpublished poems. Gibson liked these, and introduced Rob to his closest friend, Lascelles Abercrombie. Abercrombie had become the leader of the Georgians and lived in Gloucestershire, "under thatch." Gibson was planning to move there soon.

Both men prevailed upon Frost to move with his family to this charming countryside to be near them. This was not accomplished though until the spring of 1914, when they were finally able to sublet the Bungalow.

But the time they remained in Beaconsfield proved to be important for Frost. Through Gibson he met the poet Ralph Hodgson, who, in turn, introduced him to Edward Thomas, the man who was to become Rob's closest friend in England.

Putting in the Seed

You come to fetch me from my work tonight
When supper's on the table, and we'll see
If I can leave off burying the white
Soft petals fallen from the apple tree
(Soft petals, yes, but not so barren quite,
Mingled with these, smooth bean and wrinkled pea),
And go along with you ere you lose sight
Of what you came for and become like me,
Slave to a springtime passion for the earth.
How Love burns through the Putting in the Seed
On through the watching for that early birth
When, just as the soil tarnishes with weed,
The sturdy seedling with arched body comes
Shouldering its way and shedding the earth crumbs.

·11·

How Love burns through the Putting in the Seed

Much of Rob's life during these last months that they lived in Beaconsfield centered around Harold Monro's bookshop in Devonshire Street in London. In fact, Rob was able to sell Monro two poems for use in another publication of his called *Poetry and Drama*. He arranged payment for these to be the use of two rooms above the Poetry Bookshop for the interim period between the renting of the Bungalow and their move to Gloucestershire. So, once again, in the spring of 1914, the children found themselves sight-seeing in London.

When they finally took the train to the Dymock region in Gloucestershire in April, the green grass and golden daffodils they saw from the train windows were a welcome sight after the smoke and grime of London. Perhaps they thought briefly of William Wordsworth's "host of golden daffodils . . . fluttering and dancing in the breeze."

They were met at the station by a welcoming committee consisting of the Abercrombies and the Gibsons, then taken by carriage to the Abercrombies', where they were to stay until they found a cottage to their liking that they could rent.

Lascelles Abercrombie was the first of the Georgian poets to move to Dymock. He had arrived there in 1910, and settled into a large and ancient double cottage called "the Gallows." The house was so named because, hundreds of years before, a local character had been hanged there for poaching (illegally shooting) the king's deer. Gibson lived in a half-timbered cottage called "the Old Nailshop" at Greenway Cross.

Frost soon found a cottage nearby known as "Little Iddens." Built of black timber and whitened bricks, it was an old country cottage set in the rolling green fields between Dymock and Ledbury. It was far more rural than the Bungalow. Orchards of pear, cherry, and apple trees covered the hill behind the house. In front, the family could see the beautiful greenery of May Hill, four miles away. May Hill rose almost one thousand feet, and was topped by a circular grove of fir trees.

The three houses, "the Gallows," "the Old Nailshop," and "Little Iddens," were situated in a triangle about two miles from each other, with Dymock in the middle.

Inside Little Iddens was a tiny kitchen with an old-fashioned stove and baking oven. Rob described it years later:

> This is the thing I remember best of all—the kitchen and that stove—awful inconvenient that thing, and awful hard to get hot. I cooked on it, I even used to get down on my knees and pray to it.

Elinor, describing the cottage in a letter to her sister, said,

> The cottage . . . is about 350 years old, and all the floors downstairs are brick tiled and the beams show above. We have five rooms and the rent is only fifty dollars a year.

The children thought it was a fairyland house. They loved the narrow staircase to the second floor and the low-ceiling bedrooms, each with a window of leaded panes.

Rob quickly became part of this congregation of poets whose work had recently—and suddenly—become known and admired in England. Together they walked through this unspoiled countryside with its narrow lanes and high hedgerows, hunted ferns at night by the light of a match under the steep banks of the Leadon River, or searched for unusual flowers by day with the children. They delighted in comparing the English Ladies Tresses, Little Teasel, and Spreading Campanula with the flowers of New England.

The flowers always brought Rob back to poetry. Soon, he was considered the foremost practitioner of the Georgian period, even among the English poets. Many of the poems that would be included in *Mountain Interval,* published later in America, were written here. He would look back on this period as a "near-legendary interlude in his life, a romance such as happens to few."

There were idyllic picnics with the Gibsons and the Abercrombies on the bank of the Leadon River. Rob taught four-year-old Michael Abercrombie how to make a stone skip across the water. He showed all the children how to make a big splash with a little object, and a little splash with a big object. With his jackknife he carved toys for them.

Elinor wrote, again to her sister,

> I wish I could make you feel what a lovely country this is. When we first came, the meadows were covered with yellow daffodils and the cuckoo had just begun to sing. . . . The pastures here are so rich that they are just as green as the mowing and wheat fields, and they are separated by dark green hedges and bordered by huge elms. Great flocks of sheep and herds of cows are everywhere. From a hill about four miles away, one can see the Severn River winding along, and the mountains of Wales in the distance.

A month after their arrival in Gloucestershire, on May 15, 1914, *North of Boston* was published. It was twenty years earlier—almost to the day—that "My Butterfly" had been accepted by the *Independent.* Robert Frost had just turned forty.

The Frosts began to have a steady stream of visitors at Little Iddens. The first to come was Edward Thomas, whom Rob had met in London. Thomas knew and loved the Dymock region, and he took it upon himself to show it to Frost. Together they roamed the back lanes and the flower-sprinkled groves on the side of May Hill, and on up to the top. It was from here that Thomas most enjoyed pointing out to his newfound friend some of the highest peaks in Wales. Edward Thomas had been born in London, but his parents were Welsh, and he had inherited their love for the tiny country. The two men became so fond of May Hill, and walked there so often, that it can almost be looked on as a symbol of their friendship.

They hunted flowers, carrying a vasculum, or collecting tin, to put them in, and they talked of poetry. They talked of how a poet should write (as Wordsworth had said) with his eye on the object but with his ear on the speaking tones. Edward Thomas had been putting some of his feeling for this countryside into prose. He had a special sensitivity to the beauty around him, and knew all the moods of nature in the English countryside. It was Rob who showed him how, with very little alteration, his prose could become poetry. This was the key that unlocked the door on the poetry that had been stored up inside Edward for thirty-six years.

That August the Thomases moved into a neighboring farmhouse called "Oldfields"—Edward, his wife Helen, a "laughing earth-woman," and their three children with Welsh names. Mervyn, the eldest, a boy, was near Lesley's age; Bronwen, a girl, was just a little younger. The youngest was a baby girl named Myfanwy.

The men became fast friends. The women and children delighted in each other as well. The children loved Edward Thomas instantly— for his Welsh songs, for his pockets full of birds' eggs, and for his attention to them. They picked apples, they dug vegetables, they played in the meadows, and they went for long walks. All the Frosts and the Thomases dug potato patches. Potatoes were important for winter food.

They worked hard—all, that is, except Rob. While the others toiled in the blazing sun, he wandered and watched and supervised, playfully seeing to it that they did their jobs properly. They did not object. They knew a poem might be happening in him.

In the evening they would all gather in a barely furnished room in Little Iddens and, sitting on the floor in the light of only one candle, listen to the talk of Robert and Edward. If the children got hungry they would help themselves to some cold rice or an apple.

Rob, writing to Amy Lowell in 1917, described the friendship:

The closest I ever came in friendship to anyone in England or anywhere else in the world I think was Edward Thomas. . . . He more than anyone else was accessory to what I had done and was doing. We were together to the exclusion of every other person and interest all through 1914—1914 was our year. I never had, I never shall have another such year of friendship.

"The closest I ever came in friendship to anyone . . . was Edward Thomas. . . . I never had . . . such a year of friendship," Rob said. *Courtesy Jones Library, Amherst.*

Wilfred Gibson's poem "The Golden Room" (first published in the *Atlantic Monthly* for February 1926) recalls an evening at the Nailshop and vividly describes the relationship among the Frosts, the Thomases, and the others.

"The Old Nailshop" was the scene of many happy summer evenings for Rob and his new friends, the Georgian poets. *Courtesy Dartmouth College Library.*

Do you remember the still summer evening
When in the cozy cream-washed living-room
Of the Old Nailshop we all talked and laughed—
Our neighbors from the Gallows, Catherine
And Lascelles Abercrombie; Rupert Brooke;
Eleanor [sic] and Robert Frost, living awhile
At Little Iddens, who'd brought over with them
Helen and Edward Thomas? In the lamplight
We talked and laughed, but for the most part listened
While Robert Frost kept on and on
In his slow New England fashion for our delight,
Holding us with shrewd turns and racy quips,
And the rare twinkle of his grave blue eyes.

And Rob read some of his poetry to them, too. He read "Birches," and "Hyla Brook," and "Sound of Trees," written for Abercrombie, that talked about the tall trees outside the Gallows but was reminiscent also of the trees he had known in New England as a child. He may have read "Putting in the Seed," unmistakably another love poem to Elinor and calling to mind his earlier "The Pasture."

Thomas and his family had been settled next door to the Frosts for only three days when they learned that England had declared war on Germany. It was August 4, 1914.

"The war is an ill wind to me," Frost wrote to Sidney Cox. "It ends for the time being the thought of publishing any more books. Our game is up . . . so we may be coming home if we can find the fare or a job to pay the fare after we get there."

And then, in another letter to Cox:

> I should awfully like a quiet job in a small college where
> I should be allowed to teach something a little new on
> the technique of writing and where I should have some
> honor (just a little bit) for what I suppose myself to have
> done in poetry. Well, but I mustn't dream.

Rob knew in his heart he would have to go home. Edward Thomas knew that as much as he would love to go with the Frosts and settle near them in New Hampshire, he would never accomplish this. He felt called to enlist in the English army and fight for all that England stood for.

At the end of August the Thomases left for home. An idyllic month of friendship came to an end. The memory of what they had shared, and the knowledge that they would probably never again experience the beauty and closeness of this one month, made the parting even more difficult for Edward and Rob than it might have been.

Soon after the Thomases had departed, Rob accepted the Abercrombies' invitation to share the cottage at the Gallows with them. Here, at last, Elinor's long-standing wish to "live under thatch" finally came true. The two families lived casually, cooking and eating most of their meals outdoors on the terrace or in the garden, and reading poetry aloud. Catherine Abercrombie and Elinor Frost enjoyed each other, and shared the feeling that the best way to handle housework was to avoid it. Catherine admired Elinor's imperturbability—nothing seemed to bother her. "She kept her precious metal coffeepot going all day on the stove, and imbibed more coffee in a day than I did in a month."

But there were problems and tensions between Rob and Elinor during this time. "The Thatch," written many years later, hints at them:

> *Out alone in the winter rain,*
> *Intent on giving and taking pain.*
> *But never was I far out of sight*
> *Of a certain upper-window light.*
> *The light was what it was all about:*
> *I would not go in till the light went out;*
> *It would not go out till I came in.*
> *Well, we should see which one would win,*
> *We should see which one would be first to yield.*

But clashes are often intensified by caring.

With the coming of the winter months the Frosts began to see their friends going off to the front, or into war work. The children were getting homesick again, and when the submarine blockade tightened around England, Rob and Elinor decided they had better return to the United States before they were unable to do so.

After considerable difficulty, Rob booked passage on the United States line SS *St. Paul,* scheduled to sail from Liverpool at midnight on February 13, 1915. They made plans to take Mervyn Thomas with them. He would live with relatives in Alstead, New Hampshire.

As the blacked-out ship made its way out of the harbor, the *Lusitania* sailed alongside. Two British warships escorted them around Ireland, watching for German mines and submarines. After the first night they were able to relax somewhat, but the children learned quickly to wear life preservers and to participate in lifeboat drills. The portholes were blacked out at night.

Elinor and Rob, wrapped up in old shawls and sitting together in their deck chairs, talked of what they had accomplished—of Rob's "epoch-making" book, of their new friends, and of their hopes for the future.

They decided to buy a new farm in Franconia, New Hampshire, high enough in the White Mountains to escape from hay fever. They hoped to be able to raise vegetables and think about what they had done, and what they would do. It was the memory of the people and places in New Hampshire that had made them homesick while in England, and they knew they had to return there. They hoped to rent rooms again at the Lynch farm in Bethlehem, until they could find a place of their own.

They had no money, and they were concerned with how they would earn a living at home. Mrs. Nutt had paid Rob no royalties, nor had she told him of the specific arrangements she had made with the publishing firm of Henry Holt and Company in America. Mrs. Nutt seemed to feel it was enough to publish a little-known poet. To pay him seemed superfluous.

They landed in New York on a cold, bleak winter day. It was Washington's Birthday. No one was there to welcome them. They headed uptown, a small band of weary travelers, carrying their own luggage. They were planning to take the Fall River boat to New England that evening. At that time, it was the cheapest way to travel. On their way uptown they stopped at a newsstand to buy a newspaper. There, staring up at them, was a copy of a new magazine, *New Republic,* for February 20, 1915. Inside, Elinor discovered, was a three-column review of *North of Boston* written by Amy Lowell, the American poet and leader of the Imagists. A footnote indicated "by permission of Henry Holt and Company."

Rob quickly settled his family in the Grand Central Terminal waiting room, then walked to the offices of Henry Holt and Company at 34 West Thirty-third Street.

Years later, Alfred Harcourt, Holt's editor-in-chief at the time, would give a vivid description of that day. He looked up from his desk to see a handsome man of medium height, with striking blue eyes, light tousled hair, and an extraordinarily sensitive mouth standing in the doorway.

"I am Robert Frost," the man said.

And so began a publishing relationship that was to last for the remainder of his life.

In the Home Stretch

. . . .
. . . It's a day's work
To empty one house of all household goods
And fill another with 'em fifteen miles away,
Although you do no more than dump them down.''

"Dumped down in paradise we are and happy.''

"It's all so much what I have always wanted,
I can't believe it's what you wanted, too.''

"Shouldn't you like to know?''

                                "I'd like to know
If it is what you wanted, then how much
You wanted it for me.''

                        "A troubled conscience!
You don't want me to tell if *I* don't know.''

"I don't want to find out what can't be known.
But who first said the word to come?''

                                "My dear,
It's who first thought the thought. You're searching, Joe,
For things that don't exist; I mean beginnings.
Ends and beginnings—there are no such things.
There are only middles.''

. . . .

·12·

Dumped down in paradise we are and happy

It was approximately two weeks before Rob finally joined his family in New Hampshire.

Elinor took the children "home" while their father remained in New York to meet the members of the Poetry Society and the editors of the *New Republic,* all of whom were anxious to meet him.

No doubt Elinor would have preferred the excitement of literary luncheons in New York, but it fell to her to care for the children and to help them understand that their father's life was tied first and foremost to poetry.

When his New York business was completed, Rob impulsively decided to visit his sister Jeanie before starting for New Hampshire. Deciding to surprise her, he traveled by train the 150 miles from New York to Wildwood, New Jersey, where Jeanie had been teaching when she had last written to him in England. When he arrived there, though, he learned that Jeanie had been dismissed from her job. The nervous instability that had troubled Jeanie since childhood made it hard for her to hold any teaching position for more than a year. Wildwood was no exception. Jeanie was teaching now in the little coal mining town of South Fork, Pennsylvania, near Pittsburgh, three hundred miles from Wildwood.

In spite of the distance, Rob made the trip and found his sister. Her happiness at seeing him, and her obvious gratitude for the en-

Jeanie Frost in her early twenties. *Courtesy Dartmouth College Library.*

couragement and advice that Rob gave her, made him all the more pleased that he had taken the time and the trouble to find her.

But Rob was still not ready to return to New Hampshire and his family. He went from Pennsylvania to Lawrence, Massachusetts, where he arranged for an advance payment on his eight-hundred-dollar annuity, usually forthcoming in July. A letter to his old friend Sidney Cox dated March 13 reveals the main reason for his stopover in Lawrence:

> When I got to Lawrence, where I could ask for money
> (and might or might not get it) I had less than fifty cents
> left in my pocket.

A two-hundred-dollar advance was granted. Rob stayed on in Lawrence, visiting friends and even stopping in to see some of his old high school teachers. One of them convinced him to "say" a few of his own poems to her class.

From Lawrence he traveled to Boston, presumably for a few hours, to see Ellery Sedgwick, editor of the *Atlantic Monthly*. For years the *Atlantic* had been rejecting his poems, and Rob was anxious to see what would happen now.

Sedgwick so enjoyed talking to Rob, or, more accurately, listening to Rob talk, that he asked him to be a guest at a small dinner party he was giving at his home that evening. It was here, at what he later referred to as a "cut-glass dinner," that Rob met the Harvard professor of philosophy Ernest Hocking and his wife, Agnes. They were to become fast friends.

Ernest Hocking wrote an account of this meeting that typifies the kind of relationship Rob often made:

> We had little chance to talk, at this dinner. . . . We had to leave early for a Lowell Lecture. Shortly after, at a railway station in Boston, my wife spied R. F. and spoke to him, saying that she had regretted not having asked him to tea. "When do you want me?" he said. "This afternoon." "I will be there." He came, and we began talking; he stayed the night, he stayed the next day and the next night. . . . We had a great time. In three days' time, we had done a fair two-years' job of ripening friendship.

Although Frost had with him only the clothes he was wearing, he accepted also an invitation from Amy Lowell to attend a small dinner party at her home on the Monday evening that he left the Hockings'. It was only after this meeting that he was finally ready to return to the warm welcome awaiting him at the Lynch farm in Bethlehem—and to the joy of a reunion with his family.

🍂

He enjoyed exploring the area once again with his children. He loved the snow piled high about the house—snow that had been rain during his English winters. Now, on snowshoes and skis borrowed from the Lynches, he accompanied the children on adventures in the region they loved as much as he.

He became reacquainted with the New Hampshire farmers—with their way of life, their speech. He liked it when

> *The city had withdrawn itself*
> *And left at last the country to the country.*

As the snow began to thaw he took the children tramping through the mud looking for a farm to buy for the family.

And out of this came:

> *To think to know the country and not know*
> *The hillside on the day the sun lets go*
> *Ten million silver lizards out of snow!*
> *As often as I've seen it done before*
> *I can't pretend to tell the way it's done.*
> *It looks as if some magic of the sun*
> *Lifted the rug that bred them on the floor*
> *And the light breaking on them made them run.*

Even as he enjoyed the area, though, he kept thinking that had magazines such as the *Atlantic* bought some of his poems the year before when he had sent them from England, he might have earned much money: " . . . at magazine rates there is about a thousand dollars' worth of poetry in *North of Boston* that I might have had last winter if people who love me now had loved me then."

Eventually in April, Rob found exactly the farm he was looking for. One day, out walking with Lesley on a hill road about a mile outside of Franconia Village, he suddenly came upon a house facing a spectacular view of the White Mountains, dominated by the rocky peaks of the Lafayette Range.

"This is it," he said to Lesley, then walked across the lawn to a man out "raking up after winter." Rob went straight to the point: "You wouldn't want to sell me this place, would you?" he asked.

The owner, Willis E. Herbert, whose grandfather had built the house, was amused by Rob's approach. He happened to want a larger farm that was available a half-mile up the road, so if Frost were willing to pay a thousand dollars, he would move in a hurry. The deal was closed with a handshake, and no down payment.

Soon after, Herbert saw Robert Frost's picture in a Boston newspaper and learned that Frost was a poet. One day he visited Rob at the Lynches', told him he'd heard he was "somebody," and wouldn't he pay a hundred dollars more? Frost agreed.

Although the house was tiny and had neither a bathroom nor a furnace, Elinor and the children liked it immediately. The water came from an uphill spring and was fed into the house by gravity. There were a small barn, a hayfield and a pasture, woodlots with many different kinds of trees, and a sugar maple orchard with a sugar house.

The Frosts had not yet moved into the house when Rob received the first of the long line of honors he was to receive throughout the rest of his life. The Phi Beta Kappa Society at Tufts College asked him to read some of his poems at its annual meeting on May 5, 1915. Along with this invitation came another one from the Boston Authors' Club requesting that he speak at a luncheon there on the same day.

Rob was delighted on two counts. First, his poems were finally winning the acclaim he had dreamed of since he had begun writing. Then, too, this was a way to earn money for the support of his family. But Elinor did not see it that way. She begged him not to go, and accused him of buying attention and flattery at the expense of time and energy that he needed for writing more poems. She argued that she wanted him to be a private person. She resented having to share him with the public.

Elinor herself was a quiet intellectual. She had almost a desperate calm about her. There was a kind of melancholy— as though she had paid a price for protecting her husband's genius.

Rob knew, though, that he had to go through with it. He knew he had to speak at both meetings in spite of Elinor's pleas, and in spite of his own misgivings. He remembered well his inability to read "The Tuft of Flowers" before the men's league in Derry nine years before.

But on May 5, as he faced his first "town-and-gown" audience, no one listening could have guessed at the fear and nervousness hidden inside him. He read three as yet unpublished poems that had been in his pocket since England: "Birches," "The Road Not Taken," and "The Sound of Trees." The critics who wrote about the event in the newspaper the next day spoke of "the simplicity of his manner, the sincerity of his voice, and the beauty of his three poems." But Elinor had not accompanied him.

In spite of the discord at home, much good was to come of the sojourn in Boston. Rob met the poet and critic Louis Untermeyer, with whom he had corresponded, and who was to become a dear friend. Another meeting with William Stanley Braithwaite, whom he had originally met on his first visit to Boston in March, gave him the opportunity to explain to the poetry editor of the *Boston Evening*

Transcript his own theory of poetry. Braithwaite published the material in an article in the *Transcript*. This was the first time that Frost's theories appeared in print.

> What we do get in life and miss so often in literature is the sentence sounds that underlie the words. Words in themselves do not convey meaning. . . . If we go back far enough we will discover that the sound of sense existed before words, that something in the voice or vocal gesture made primitive man convey a meaning to his fellow before the race developed a more elaborate and concrete symbol of communication in language.

A few months before, writing to Sidney Cox from England, Rob had said, "We value the seeing eye already. Time we said something about the hearing ear—the ear that calls up vivid sentence forms. We write of things we see and we write in accents we hear," and, "You recognize the sentence sound in this: You, you——! It is so strong that if you hear it as I do you have to pronounce the two yous differently."

Even as a young boy growing up in Lawrence, he had always liked to stop and listen to people talking. His ear for speech might be compared to the "perfect pitch" of a musician. He once said that he liked people for their voice tones before he liked them for themselves.

On the morning after he delivered his two talks, Frost paid another visit to Ellery Sedgwick. When Sedgwick asked Frost if he had any poems with him, Frost replied,

> "I am not the kind of poet who goes around with poems in my pocket. But, as it happens, I have three right here that I've been reading at Tufts College."
> "Let me have them."
> "Are you sure you want them?"
> "Yes."

Frost said later that it was one of the best strokes in his favor that he ever had. It made "Birches," in particular, one of his best-known poems.

Many invitations to read his poems came from academic institutions following his reading at Tufts. In a period of two weeks, from January 13 to 26, 1916, Rob spoke at Abbot Academy in Andover, Massachusetts; at Dartmouth College in Hanover, New Hampshire; at the Dartmouth Alumni Association meeting in Boston; at the Poetry Society of America in New York City; and at Exeter in New Hampshire.

Elinor resented them all. She saw the strain on Rob of these "barding ventures" and tried to convince him that his first loyalty should be to his poetry. She alone knew the trembling and the anguish caused him by standing in front of a large audience—either to read his poems or to explain his theories. She alone knew the courage it took to overcome this, and the actual illness it often provoked—the pain in his head, in his stomach, in his heart—that took a week to recuperate from.

Whenever he returned from a reading trip, she would greet his fatigue and grouchiness with silence, help him to bed, and then complain to the children, "Your father *must* give this up. His health is failing. His life is being ruined. His poetry is suffering. It *can't* go on!" To Elinor, the gains of the readings clearly did not offset the losses.

Only little Marjorie, at that time, seemed to approve of her father. She told Mrs. Lynch that Rob was a good one to write poetry and to bring up children.

Early in June 1915, Ellery Sedgwick sent Rob a check for fifty-five dollars for the three poems he had left with him and told him that they would be published in the August issue of the *Atlantic*. This issue would also contain an article in praise of Robert Frost by the highly respected English critic Edward Garnett. It had the hoped-for effect. By the end of the summer *North of Boston* was a best-seller.

Meanwhile in June, the Frosts had moved from the Lynches' into the farm they had purchased in Franconia. It was a happy time for all of them. Rob loved playing at farming. He enjoyed the work, he said, because so much of it could be neglected. Often, he simply sat on the porch, looking out over the valley of farmland that stretched toward magnificent Lafayette Mountain in the distance—or making poems on the ever-present pad in his lap—while Elinor and the children planted the vegetable garden.

He began each day—never early—by studying the clouds and the mountains to determine what the weather would be like. He needed

The Frost family in Bridgewater, New Hampshire, 1915. Left to right, front row: Marjorie, Carol; middle row: Lesley, Irma; back row: Elinor, Robert. *Courtesy Plymouth State College Library, New Hampshire.*

rain for their newly planted seeds, but not enough to drown them.

The children, happier than they had been in a long time, went to school in the village and made friends there. Their father quickly gained the respect of the townspeople and was elected president of the PTA. The children found a swimming hole near the house where all but Marjorie learned to swim. She was afraid of deep water. They played baseball with their father, they went berrying together, and they helped him transplant wild flowers, trees, and shrubs from the woods and meadows to their own backyard, or to the side of the brook that flowed from their spring.

Each spring all the Frosts tapped their own maple trees. They collected the sap, carried tin pails of it to the sugar house, and boiled it down into either maple syrup or sugar.

In wintertime, dressed like an old tramp, Rob often walked alone, occasionally stopping at a house along the way to say, "Do I smell coffee?" The natives of Franconia all liked Rob. They liked to gossip with him and to feed him, and it was on these solitary walks that "the pang that made poetry" for him was often at work. Much of *Mountain Interval* was to be poetry that came as he walked the Franconia hills.

A TIME TO TALK

When a friend calls to me from the road
And slows his horse to a meaning walk,
I don't stand still and look around
On all the hills I haven't hoed,
And shout from where I am, "What is it?"
No, not as there is a time to talk.
I thrust my hoe in the mellow ground,
Blade-end up and five feet tall,
And plod: I go up to the stone wall
For a friendly visit.

But there were worries also. In the fall of 1916 Elinor was ill, and pregnant again. She had developed a heart condition and had been warned that having any more children could be dangerous. This was her seventh pregnancy. Rob was truly frightened, and when Elinor suffered a miscarriage, he was much relieved.

"We are still six in the family, no more and, thank God, no less," he wrote to Lascelles Abercrombie in England. And to Louis Untermeyer he wrote, "We are lucky in all being still alive. I am nurse, cook, and chambermaid to the crowd. . . ."

On impulse, and knowing it was an extravagance he could ill afford, he bought Elinor a piano, then wrote "The Investment":

Over back where they speak of life as staying
("You couldn't call it living, for it ain't"),
There was an old, old house renewed with paint,
And in it a piano loudly playing.

Out in the plowed ground in the cold a digger,
Among unearthed potatoes standing still,
Was counting winter dinners, one a hill,
With half an ear to the piano's vigor.

All that piano and new paint back there,
Was it some money suddenly come into?
Or some extravagance young love had been to?
Or old love on an impulse not to care—

Not to sink under being man and wife,
But get some color and music out of life?

In June 1916, just one year after he was honored by Tufts College, Rob was asked by Harvard to be their Phi Beta Kappa poet at commencement. George Herbert Palmer, retired professor of philosophy, invited Rob to be his guest for the weekend and to bring Elinor with him.

Elinor did attend, and the weekend was a memorable one. His poems "The Bonfire" and "The Ax-helve" were well received, and he returned to Franconia in a good mood, ready to complete his next book.

Mountain Interval appeared in November 1916. It represented exactly what its name implied. Its dedication:

TO YOU

WHO LEAST NEED REMINDING

that before the interval of the South Branch under black mountains, there was another interval, the Upper at Plymouth, where we walked in spring beyond the covered bridge; but that the first interval of all was the old farm, our brook interval, so called by the man we had it from in sale

pointed the way back into the past for its sources and proved again that though Rob and Elinor were different in their natures, they were still a pair—alike and together even in their differences. Rob was to say, years later, "after making her first big resistance . . . to be swept into my good-for-nothing life [Elinor] accepted everything." And then, in a letter to a friend, "Pretty nearly every one of my poems will be found to be about her if rightly read."

The affectionate banter of the married couple in his poem "In the Home Stretch" in *Mountain Interval* seems to mirror Rob and Elinor's life together. Their many moves, accompanied by the necessary packing and unpacking, are reflected in its lines. But always, they considered themselves "dumped down in paradise we are and happy."

Just one month after the publication of *Mountain Interval,* on a cold December afternoon, Rob received an invitation from Amherst College. Stark Young, a member of the English department at Amherst, visited Rob in Franconia to speak for President Alexander Meiklejohn and offer to Frost an appointment as full professor of English at Amherst, starting in January 1917. The salary would be two thousand dollars and Frost would be free to make readings at other schools—to "bard around" as he called it—to supplement his income.

Rob was in a dilemma. If he once again began to teach, would he lose his ability to make poems? He thought back to the letter he had written to Sidney Cox from England in 1914—the letter in which he confided his dream of a job in a small college where he could teach his theories of writing and have "some honor for what I suppose myself to have done in poetry." He liked and respected the young President Meiklejohn of Amherst—only two years older than he. He liked the direction in which he was leading Amherst.

Frost also saw the opportunity to get his family away from the twenty-five-degree-below-zero weather of Franconia winter. Both he and Carol were constantly sick during the winter. Rob and Elinor talked it over often into the night, and finally he made the decision. But for "just one term," he told Elinor. "We can stand that."

A letter from President Meiklejohn to Frost, soon after he accepted, indicated the feeling of the Amherst community:

> This morning at the chapel service I read "The Road Not Taken" and then told the boys about your coming. They applauded vigorously and were evidently much delighted at the prospect. I can assure you of an eager and hearty welcome by the community.

But his poetry would never be the same again. The connection between the poems and the land that seemed a vital part of his creating was no longer available to him.

The Runaway

Once when the snow of the year was beginning to fall,
We stopped by a mountain pasture to say, "Whose colt?"
A little Morgan had one forefoot on the wall,
The other curled at his breast. He dipped his head
And snorted at us. And then he had to bolt.
We heard the miniature thunder where he fled,
And we saw him, or thought we saw him, dim and gray,
Like a shadow against the curtain of falling flakes.
"I think the little fellow's afraid of the snow.
He isn't winter-broken. It isn't play
With the little fellow at all. He's running away.
I doubt if even his mother could tell him, 'Sakes,
It's only weather.' He'd think she didn't know!
Where is his mother? He can't be out alone."
And now he comes again with clatter of stone,
And mounts the wall again with whited eyes
And all his tail that isn't hair up straight.
He shudders his coat as if to throw off flies.
"Whoever it is that leaves him out so late,
When other creatures have gone to stall and bin,
Ought to be told to come and take him in."

·13·

He's running away

And so began again the pattern that his life seemed to take. "Three things have followed me, writing, teaching and a little farming," he once said. "I get a queer unhappiness when I don't have a little land to farm. Writing, teaching, farming—three strands of my life."

From the start, the Amherst community loved him. At his first public reading there this farmer, "sturdily built, wearing rumpled clothes and a celluloid collar, with unruly brown hair, blunt features, and eyes of seafarer's blue that had a way of magically lighting up," charmed his audience.

This pattern also would supply the adventure and change that all the family, except Marjorie, seemed to need, and to thrive on. But they themselves did not seem to change:

> *They would not find me changed from him they knew—*
> *Only more sure of all I thought was true.*

The day they moved into the house on Dana Street that they had been able to sublet, furnished, was bleak and cold. Mrs. Otto Manthey-Zorn, wife of a German professor at Amherst, watched from her window in the house next door as a gypsy band of youngsters, animals, and chickens in coops came tumbling out of a battered old car. They had a desperate, lost look about them.

Anxious to be helpful, she ran across the yard to see what she might do. Elinor's beautiful, classic face encircled by long braids was distressed. The home had no blankets and, "He catches pneumonia so easily," she whispered. A long and beautiful friendship began when Mrs. Manthey-Zorn ran back to her house, pulled the blankets off her own bed for her new neighbors, and decided that she and her husband could sleep under their coats that night.

Elinor and the children were happy in Amherst. Elinor enjoyed her newfound friend, life in the Amherst community, and having all four of the children enrolled in public school.

Lesley, of all the children, was perhaps the happiest. She was enrolled in the classical course at the high school and clearly relished following in her father's footsteps. Her reading of the *Aeneid* in Latin in her class brought recognition to her and to her poet father. Carol, though, eclipsed by his father and dominated by his older sister, refused to work hard at school.

But for Rob, there was no time to write. By the time the term was over he realized that he had not submitted one poem for publication to any magazine. He was bringing excitement into his classes, however, inspiring the boys to new ideas. And he obviously loved it. Why else was he frequently found trailing troops of boys in the Amherst hills, or reading poetry to them in his parlor at home at midnight?

His teaching appeared to be informal. He was always late for class, yet angry if the students did not wait for him. He much preferred sprawling out on a couch at home to sitting in a chair in class for "teaching," and this he often did: "I don't teach," he once said. "I don't know how. I talk and I have the boys talk." The boys were to read some of the minor authors—"The fellows who didn't blow their trumpets so loudly but who nevertheless sounded a beautiful note."

He believed very strongly that the only education worth anything was self-education. He said at Amherst that "some are self-made outside of college; some are self-made in college; but all are self-made if made to any purpose.

"Everyday I feel bound to save my consistency by advising my pupils to leave school. Then if they insist on coming to school it is not my fault: I can teach with a clear conscience."

Even Rob's posture seemed symbolic. He would sit slumped down in a chair, his legs spread out in front of him in his comfortable old-fashioned shoes. Every now and then his broad, hairy fingers would rub the blunt tip of his nose, or mess his thick graying hair.

But he gave much of himself to an eager student. He did not care how much they read or wrote. He cared only how they *thought* about what they had read:

> I want you putting two and two together, and I don't
> care a hurrah for anything else. . . . As long as I stay
> around the college that will be my reason for staying.
> I have run away, you know. I ran away twice and I
> walked away a good many times.

His casual manner belied a concentration on form. He insisted that he never planned an hour with a class. As he walked to class he would think of something to use as a nucleus, a beginning. Generally, before the end of the class hour, he and the class had brought something to a shape.

He told the boys, "The chief reason for going to school is to get the impression fixed for life that there is a book side to everything. We go to college to be given one more chance to learn to read in case we haven't learned in high school. Once we have learned to read, the rest can be trusted to add itself on to us." He knew from his own experience that "the ripples a teacher makes in a life's pond never stop! It's a kind of immortality, isn't it? Writing. Yes, and teaching!"

And so, in spite of the fact that he was not altogether happy at Amherst, that he dreaded campus politics and, much against his will, found himself drawn into them, he accepted the invitation to remain another year. This time the salary would be $2500, again with time free for "barding."

During his first spring at Amherst, in an atmosphere of books and learning, of walking and talking, of sunshine and blossoming shrubs, Rob once again became:

ACQUAINTED WITH THE NIGHT

I have been one acquainted with the night.
I have walked out in rain—and back in rain.
I have outwalked the furthest city light.

I have looked down the saddest city lane.
I have passed by the watchman on his beat
And dropped my eyes, unwilling to explain.

I have stood still and stopped the sound of feet
When far away an interrupted cry
Came over houses from another street,

But not to call me back or say good-by;
And further still at an unearthly height
One luminary clock against the sky

Proclaimed the time was neither wrong nor right.
I have been one acquainted with the night.

Once again, he knew despair. In April Rob learned that his friend Edward Thomas had been killed at Vimy Ridge, near Arras, in the British spring offensive. Had Rob's tender little war poem, written when Edward had come home to his wife and children at Christmastime, 1916, just before he left for the front in France, been a foreshadowing of Edward's death?

They sent him back to her. . . .

. . . . .

the same
Grim giving to do over for them both.
She dared no more than ask him with her eyes
How was it with him for a second trial.
And with his eyes he asked her not to ask.
They had given him back to her, but not to keep.

Rob could not hide his feelings, nor did he try, when he wrote to Edward's widow:

He was the bravest and best and dearest man you and I have ever known . . . he is all yours. But you must let me crying cry for him as if he were *almost* all mine too.

Later he wrote to Edward Garnett, "E. T. was the only brother I ever had. . . . I hadn't a plan for the future that didn't include him."

In June Rob took his family home to Franconia for a summer of rejuvenation. Then in the fall of 1917 they returned to Amherst to live, this time in the town of West Pelham, several miles from the campus. "But walking was like breathing to Frost."

He often walked home with his friend in the department of English, George Whicher. Sometimes they made the trip between Amherst and Pelham four ways in one evening, talking all the while . . . with the streetlights turned off long before they were finished.

He continued inviting the boys to drop by his home at ten and eleven at night, to sprawl out on a couch in the sitting room and to read aloud from various poets. Occasionally, the boys would catch a glimpse of Elinor, described by one of them at that time as "one of the few completely beautiful women I have ever known."

It was at about this time that Amy Lowell published her *Tendencies in Modern American Poetry*. This was a volume of critical/biographical essays of six American poets. One of the best essays was the one on Robert Frost. She described him as a man "all compounded . . . of the granite and gentians of our Northern mountains," and "His eyes may see the soft rounded English country . . . but the lines etched upon his heart are the articulate outlines of rock and hemlock." But she upset Rob when she wrote about Elinor. He expressed his annoyance in a letter to Louis Untermeyer:

> I really like least her mistake about Elinor. That's an unpardonable attempt to do her as the conventional help meet of genius. . . . She has resisted every inch of the way my efforts to get money. She is not too sure that she cares about my reputation. . . . She always knew that I was a good poet, but that was between her and me, and there I think she would have liked it if it had remained at least until we were dead. I don't know that I can make you understand that kind of a person. Catch her getting any kind of satisfaction out of what her housekeeping may have done to feed a poet! Rats! She hates housekeeping. She has worked because the work has piled on top of her. But she hasn't pretended to like house-work even for my sake. . . . She's especially wary of honors that derogate from the poetic life she fancies us living. What a cheap common unindividualized picture Amy makes of her.

❧

When Rob wrote "The Runaway" for the boys at Amherst, they knew the little colt in the poem was really the runaway in the poet and in themselves. *Photo by Lawrence H. Bober, courtesy Jones Library, Amherst.*

Amherst at that time was part college, part military camp, and the boys were confused. Rob brought a sense of stability and of peace to them, a sense of value to their thinking. But he was beginning to feel restless himself. When the boys asked him for a poem for their June 1918 issue of the *Amherst Monthly*, he gave them "The Runaway."

The boys knew immediately that the poet was speaking of them—that the little colt of the poem was really the runaway in the poet and the runaway in themselves. And they loved Rob even more.

Then, early in 1920, the runaway in Rob won out once again, and he decided to leave Amherst at the end of the term and to move back to Franconia in March 1920. His decision to leave the safe harbor of Amherst for the cold of the Franconia mountains may have seemed foolish. But it gave to Rob the chance to read Wordsworth and Shakespeare and Homer again. It gave him the chance to relax and reflect. A calmness that had been missing returned to his face. He published ten poems that year, the nucleus of his next book, *New Hampshire*.

Bright-eyed Marjorie, in whose poetry Rob saw immense promise, particularly loved Franconia. She loved to curl up with a book in front of the fire in the farmhouse while the snow swirled outside. She loved to go sledding with her sisters and brother. But most of all, she loved to run free in the snow-covered mountains. Her own poem "Franconia" illustrates her free spirit:

> *Long, long ago a little child,*
> *Bareheaded in the snow,*
> *Lay back against the wind—and smiled,*
> *Then let her footsteps blow.*
>
> *Lighter than leaves they blew about,*
> *Until she sank to rest*
> *Down where no wind could blow her out,*
> *Deep in a mountain nest.*
>
> *And to this day she's smiling there*
> *With eyes alert and wild,*
> *For she has lived on mountain air*
> *And stayed a little child.*

They endured a bitter cold winter. One day when Elinor wrote to her friend Harriet Whicher at Amherst, telling her that it was twenty below zero that morning, Rob added "A Correction":

> *When we told you minus twenty*
> *Here this morning, that seemed plenty.*
> *We are trying to be modest*
> *(said he spitting in the sawdust),*
> *And moreover did our guessing*
> *By the kitchen stove while dressing.*
> *Come to dress and make a sortie,*
> *What we found was minus forty.*

The Whichers were so delighted with the little poem that they framed it and hung it in their study.

By the end of 1920 Rob began to feel uncomfortable in Franconia too. His neighbors resented the sophisticated teachers and authors who drove through their little village to find Frost's house. He seemed to be living in two different worlds . . . the world of the country farmer, and the world of academia. He loved Franconia. It had been a haven during hay-fever season. Like the Derry farm, this place had come to be home. But he knew he couldn't stay even though, as he said to his friend Sidney Cox, "They say when you run away from a place it is yourself you are running away from and that goes with you and is the first thing you meet in the next place you turn up."

> So one morning in September (1920) I just piled them in the old car and by night we had a new roof over our heads—the entrancing stone house we'd admired in South Shaftsbury, Vermont.

By now Rob and Elinor had moved so many times that they had learned to use packing crates as bookcases. These could be moved from one house to another without having to be unpacked. They were simply set one on top of the other against the wall in their new home.

Rob's feelings about this move were revealed in a letter to his friend Louis Untermeyer just before he moved. "Gee, I'm blue about this move to new scenes and new neighbors. Encourage me in it as you always have in all things."

After they had been living in their new home for a month, he wrote to Louis Untermeyer:

> I wasn't taken up carefully enough in Franconia nor replanted soon enough in South Shaftsbury. It has been a bad job of transplanting. I lost a lot of roots. . . . Even in the case of evergrins [*sic*] I find that the fall is *not* a favorable time for transplanting. And I'm not an evergrin.

The house they moved into was built of gray block stone from the area. It was one of only three houses of stone in the vicinity. All the others were white clapboard with green shutters. The stone, which went two thirds of the way up, had been left beautifully rough, "just as it flaked off under the quarrymen's hammers." It looked "homey," strong, cheerful, protective as it sat among maple, chestnut, elm, and apple trees at the top of a hill. It seemed almost to be fenced in by misty mountains to the north, south, east, and west. Ultimately, it became for the Frosts their own world of contentment and peace. Elinor, particularly, was happy here, and her soft brown eyes reflected it all. Later the house would become a haven for Carol.

Together, father and son planted apple seedlings, knowing full well that it would be years before any would bear fruit. They bought a thousand red pine seedlings also and planted these on a hillside they had cleared of brush. They bought a Jersey cow and brought their mare, a Morgan named Beauty, from Franconia. This last they accomplished by sending her by train to White River Junction. Then Carol met the train and rode Beauty the remaining eighty-two miles to South Shaftsbury, camping overnight. Once there, Rob found every excuse to use her—hitched to the buggy he bought for that purpose—to ride all around the countryside. Carol preferred their secondhand car for his errands.

Rob and Carol, kindred restless spirits, planted hundreds of trees together and often tramped through the Franconia hills. Here they rest against the backdrop of Lafayette Mountain, 1916. *Courtesy Dartmouth College Library.*

Stopping by Woods on a Snowy Evening

Whose woods these are I think I know.
His house is in the village, though;
He will not see me stopping here
To watch his woods fill up with snow.

My little horse must think it queer
To stop without a farmhouse near
Between the woods and frozen lake
The darkest evening of the year.

He gives his harness bells a shake
To ask if there is some mistake.
The only other sound's the sweep
Of easy wind and downy flake.

The woods are lovely, dark, and deep,
But I have promises to keep,
And miles to go before I sleep,
And miles to go before I sleep.

·14·

I have promises to keep

Rob began to accept speaking engagements at colleges again. During one of these, at Bryn Mawr College, he met Kathleen Johnston, a young student who would—years later—become very important to him. He was writing and selling poems. He wrote of his poems to Harriet Monroe, "I am cleaned out for the moment. But I am having some more at a great rate."

But he could not live on the income from the poems. So, in June 1921 he accepted an offer from President Marion Le Roy Burton of the University of Michigan in Ann Arbor to become a fellow in the creative arts for the academic year 1921–22. The title referred to what we now call "poet in residence." Rob playfully called himself "Michigan's Idle Fellow."

The fellowship provided no plan. It required nothing more than Rob's presence on the Ann Arbor campus. He would be free to write poetry, being asked only to mingle with the students and encourage those interested in writing.

Rob was excited. He saw the possibility of proving through this experience the desirability of establishing creative fellowships in all state universities. He arrived in Ann Arbor with Lesley. The rest of the family would follow shortly.

Lesley's restless spirit had prompted her to leave Wellesley after her first year there, and then Barnard, where she had spent her sophomore year. Now she had decided to spend her junior year at Michigan with her father. But she was not to complete school there either. Frost

Lesley in Spain. "I needed my [college] degree, why didn't they *make* me see it?" she said of her parents. *Courtesy Robin Hudnut.*

blamed himself: "My line of talk isn't calculated to make her like any institution." He and Elinor allowed her to leave school, and to stay for a few months with their friend Harriet Moody. Many years later, when she was a married woman with children of her own, Lesley would remark about her parents, "I needed my degree, why didn't they *make* me see it?"

An old white neoclassical house was found for the Frosts, and soon the rest of the family arrived. They were quickly caught up in a social whirl of tea parties and full-dress dinners.

Many of the faculty lived in large houses and had household help. They entertained at formal dinner parties, set elegant tables with fine china and silverware, and their wives wore lovely jewelry. While this was not Rob and Elinor's style, still they had a good time.

They made many friends. Rob loved to sit and talk, and the twinkle in his eye and the hand outstretched in friendly greeting wherever he went were proof enough that he was enjoying himself.

He never lost sight, though, of how differently he and Elinor lived. He knew all too well that Elinor had known real poverty and that she had had poverty put upon her for the sake of poetry. Sometimes Rob felt so badly about it that he wept and reproached himself bitterly.

At Michigan, he was invited by Professor Roy Cowden, adviser to the college literary magazine called *Whimsies,* to meet with its staff at Cowden's home. Rob enjoyed the informality of these meetings and the opportunity to make contact with young hopeful writers. He would sit in a dim corner of the room, far removed from the circle of students and the big wicker chair they had readied for him in their midst.

His criticisms of the manuscripts being read were always gentle. A student then described him: "The conversation of Frost sparkles, more lightly, more elusively, and is at its best in the pauses—when it is in his eyes, between words."

He arranged poetry readings on the campus by several of the celebrated writers of the "new poetry," Louis Untermeyer, Vachel Lindsay, Carl Sandburg, and Amy Lowell. When Amy Lowell declined the students' original offer, Rob wrote her a quiet note asking her to reconsider. "They are children," he wrote. "They are taking a great deal on themselves." She came. When he invited Louis Untermeyer he told him, "Our art [poetry] can do more to entertain them than any other art but football."

Each one came. Rob teased Amy Lowell on stage as 2500 students listened. He quipped about Carl Sandburg, who was staying at the Frost home, "He's standing by his mirror fixing his hair so it will look as if a comb had never touched it," and when Vachel Lindsay came, Rob stayed in the background and simply enjoyed listening to him. Vachel had early gained—and kept—Frost's admiration and respect.

In June 1922, when the Frosts returned to South Shaftsbury, Rob was exhausted. Nonetheless, soon after his arrival he had "one of the great happy experiences of his poetic life." One night after everyone had gone to bed, he sat down alone at the dining-room table. His feet stretched out in front of him, in his comfortable old-fashioned shoes, he began to write a poem that had been taking shape in his mind for a while. This evening he was following a pattern that he had established back in the Derry days and continued in Beaconsfield—writing while the rest of the family slept. This time, though, he wrote straight through the night.

When Rob finally looked up he realized that he had written an entire poem in one night, "New Hampshire," a long, colloquial-satirical blank verse poem. As the sun began to rise in the east, he walked out into the early morning light. Standing on the stone steps, he looked out at the grass still wet with dew, and at the syringa bush at the edge of the front lawn, just beginning to emerge from darkness. He still couldn't quite grasp what had happened. Never before had he worked straight through until morning. But the sense of exhilaration that he felt was strange. He knew somehow that there was more in him that had to be put down on paper. What it was he didn't know. Mechanically, almost in a trance, he moved back into the house, sat down at the table where he had been writing, and "in one stroke of the pen," as he said, wrote another poem totally different from the first. Recalling the despair he had felt one Christmas seventeen years before when he was returning home alone in a driving snowstorm—penniless—he wrote:

> *The woods are lovely, dark, and deep,*
> *But I have promises to keep,*
> *And miles to go before I sleep,*
> *And miles to go before I sleep.*

"Stopping by Woods on a Snowy Evening" was to become his favorite among the lyrics. Even as he wrote it he knew it would be his "best bid for remembrance."

When he was questioned about how he wrote his poems, Rob said, "A poem is never planned beforehand. Many, many other poems of mine have been written in one stroke. Some have trouble in one spot and I may never get them right."

He sometimes thought back to the first poem of his to be published in a magazine. "My Butterfly" had been written almost thirty years before, "all at one go" at the kitchen table of the Tremont Street house in Lawrence.

On another occasion, though, he said, "I have worried quite a number of my poems into existence. But my sneaky preference remains for the ones I carried through like the stroke of a raquet, club, or headman's ax. . . . They have been the experience I couldn't help returning for more of."

He often kept poems long enough to let the paper yellow because a stanza or a line did not seem quite right. His friend Sidney Cox described this by saying, "He wooed like Jacob for a perfect phrase." He told his students to hold on to what they wrote. Using farming as his metaphor, he told them, "Refuse to be rushed to market or forum. Don't come as a product till you have turned yourself under many times."

Late in the summer of 1922, Rob agreed to accompany the children on a mountain-climbing expedition on the "Long Trail." This was a 261-mile "Footpath in the Wilderness" that had recently been completed by the Green Mountain Club across Vermont, from Massachusetts to Canada. In addition to Lesley, Carol, and Marjorie, there was a girl named Lillian LaBatt accompanying them. Lillian had shared a rented apartment with Marjorie when the two girls attended Bennington High School while the rest of the Frosts were in Michigan.

Rob did over a hundred miles of the trail with the young people. As he walked, his pleasure in botanizing was reawakened. He greeted all his favorite old flowers as friends. He even said hello out loud to some of them when he was sure no one was near enough to hear him. He studied the leaves of the trees and bushes he passed, and chewed the bark of the black birch to get the wintergreen flavor from it.

Then, after a little more than a week, a sore foot compelled him to leave the young people to continue by themselves while he attempted to get home on his own. He petulantly reported later that the children's only concern was that he leave them enough money for food for the next week. They didn't seem at all concerned about *him*.

By the time they all reassembled in South Shaftsbury, several significant things had happened. Carol announced that he and Lillian had fallen in love and were engaged to be married. And Rob had had the time and the freedom to write poetry again. This he did for the remainder of the summer.

When Rob received a telegram from President Burton of Michigan in October, inviting him to return to the university and telling him that students, faculty, regents, and citizens united in invitation, Rob could not refuse. But this time he went alone. Carol flatly refused to go. He preferred to remain on the farm. Not even Michigan's football team could lure him away from Lillian. Marjorie wanted to

Marjorie, at the time of her graduation from Bennington High School in 1923. *Courtesy Robin Hudnut.*

finish her last year at Bennington High School. Irma wanted to stay and keep house for Carol, and Lesley had made arrangements to work in a New York City bookstore. Elinor decided not to leave the children just yet. She knew that Rob's commitments to read poetry, made before the invitation had come from Michigan, would necessitate his leaving Ann Arbor for a while soon after his arrival there. She would go back with him later.

Rob attended a reception at the university and stayed with Dean Bursley for two days, meeting old friends and making plans for the new semester. He left for a brief stopover at home in South Shaftsbury, then on to speaking engagements in Vermont; Boston, Massachusetts; New Orleans, Louisiana; Austin, Dallas, Fort Worth, San Antonio, and Waco, Texas; and Columbia, Missouri. There were ten readings in fourteen days.

But in spite of the reviews citing his sense of humor, his gentleness, his whimsical sincerity, Rob returned to his new home in Michigan tired, angry, and depressed. He had a severe case of influenza—and was confined to bed for more than a week.

Elinor, having left all the children back East, tried hard to nurse him back to health and to good spirits. Soon he was caught up once again in campus life, enjoying particularly his time spent with the staff of *Whimsies.* When invitations began flowing in again for more lectures he was able to refuse them. A letter to his old friend George Whicher, who had asked him to speak at the Bread Loaf School of English that next summer, bears testimony that he was beginning to listen to Elinor:

> I had promised her [Elinor] . . . that there should be no more lecturing after April 1st this year. This was in my interest, in the interest of my writing. . . . She's right: it's time I shut up long enough to get my last poems written. At any rate right or wrong she is entitled to a voice in the matter. . . . It lets me out of having to think of money for the family as much as I was feeling I had to. . . .
>
> Forgive me my selfishness.

He did start to write again, and to assemble and arrange the poems for another volume. The choice of particular poems and the careful, imaginative arrangement of them was important to Rob. This book was an outgrowth of the excitement of having produced in one night his long, conversational "New Hampshire," and the short, lovely lyric "Stopping by Woods."

Lawrence Conrad, who had been one of Rob's favorite students at the University of Michigan and was now an instructor in rhetoric there, offered to type the manuscript of Rob's new volume of poetry. Conrad hoped to make a career of writing himself, and enjoyed his relationship with Rob.

Often as Conrad typed the poems, with Rob watching over his shoulder, the poet would take a page to the bottom of the stairs, call up to Elinor, and ask her to listen while he read something aloud. He took her decision as to which of two stanzas was better. Sometimes he would shout up, "Elinor, how did we decide to spell this word?" Elinor, in turn, was proud of the role she played. She, like William Wordsworth's wife Mary over one hundred years earlier, enjoyed contributing an occasional line or two of poetry, or offering sought-after advice: Elinor probably had not written poetry of her own since it had upset Rob when they were still in high school together.

The influence Rob had on the students at Michigan was difficult to calculate. He touched many more of the ten thousand young men and women than could actually be counted. Lawrence Conrad expressed this influence in a letter to President Burton:

> I have felt him in classrooms when he was not there at all, curbing "smartness," checking rash judgments, warring against the cheap, the silly, the spectacular. Everyone who knows him has been given a turn toward a new appreciation of hard, honest effort, of sound, sane values, of honesty and simplicity and open-mindedness.

In June Rob returned to South Shaftsbury to relax and resume work on *New Hampshire*. Lincoln MacVeagh, his friend and editor at Henry Holt, had set a summer deadline for the book. Rob knew he would meet it.

New Hampshire (his fourth book) was divided into three parts. Part one was simply the title poem, "New Hampshire." Part two Rob called "Notes." This included explanatory poems that told a story. Part three, short lyrics added for ornamentation, he called "Grace Notes." "Stopping by Woods" was part of this section.

Another little lyric that appeared in "Grace Notes" was "Dust of Snow." Written all in one sentence, it was a study in blacks and whites that might also have been a subtle self-portrait. Perhaps it served to restore his self-confidence and to lessen his ever-present fear that the period of his best writing had ended:

> *The way a crow*
> *Shook down on me*
> *The dust of snow*
> *From a hemlock tree*
>
> *Has given my heart*
> *A change of mood*
> *And saved some part*
> *Of a day I had rued.*

New Hampshire, considered by many to be Rob's best book, was noteworthy on several counts. It was the first of Rob's work to be illustrated. J. J. Lankes did woodcut illustrations of the poems. And the newly established Pulitzer Prize for poetry was awarded to it as the best book of poems published in America in 1923.

Robert Frost had certainly "lodged a few poems where they would be hard to get rid of." The gamble he had taken when he first left the security of a teaching job in Plymouth to sail for England was now truly justified. His wistful hope, expressed to Susan Hayes Ward back in 1894, that he might someday have a volume of his poems, had been fulfilled full measure.

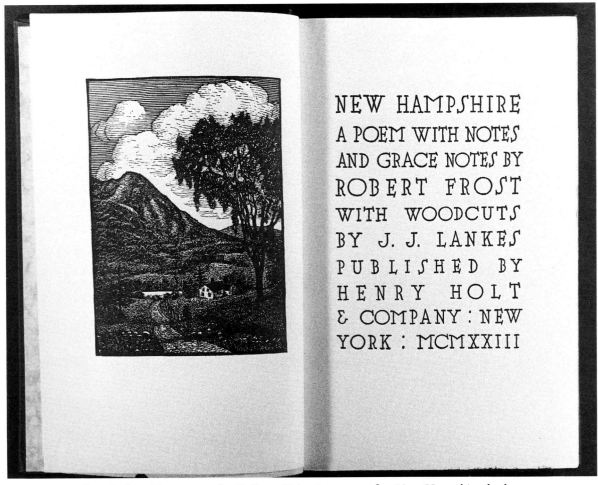

When Robert Frost won the Pulitzer Prize in poetry for *New Hampshire,* he knew he had "lodged a few poems where they would be hard to get rid of." The J. J. Lankes woodcut for the title page of *New Hampshire. Photo by Lawrence H. Bober, courtesy J. J. Lankes.*

West-Running Brook

"Fred, where is north?"

               "North? North is there, my love.
The brook runs west."

            "West-Running Brook then call it."
(West-Running Brook men call it to this day.)
"What does it think it's doing running west

When all the other country brooks flow east
To reach the ocean? It must be the brook
Can trust itself to go by contraries
The way I can with you—and you with me—
Because we're—we're—I don't know what we are.
What are we?"

        "Young or new?"

                "We must be something.
We've said we two. Let's change that to we three.
As you and I are married to each other,
We'll both be married to the brook. We'll build
Our bridge across it, and the bridge shall be
Our arm thrown over it asleep beside it.
Look, look, it's waving to us with a wave
To let us know it hears me."

. . . .

"Speaking of contraries, see how the brook
In that white wave runs counter to itself.
It is from that in water we were from
Long, long before we were from any creature.
. . . .
It has this throwing backward on itself
So that the fall of most of it is always
Raising a little, sending up a little.
Our life runs down in sending up the clock.

The brook runs down in sending up our life.
The sun runs down in sending up the brook.
And there is something sending up the sun.
It is this backward motion toward the source,
Against the stream, that most we see ourselves in,
The tribute of the current to the source.
It is from this in nature we are from.
It is most us."
                         "Today will be the day
You said so."
                         "No, today will be the day
You said the brook was called West-Running Brook."

"Today will be the day of what we both said."

·15·

To go by contraries

During that summer of 1923 Rob's feelings for Amherst, the small college that had first recognized his ability as a teacher, were stirred once again. The brilliant President Meiklejohn was dismissed at commencement 1923, and Frost was distressed, both for his friend Meiklejohn and for the students and faculty, who were divided over the move. But Acting President George Daniel Olds prevailed upon Rob to return to Amherst as professor of English, and to teach a course in philosophy as well. Rob knew the security a professorship would offer his family.

So once again he became "a bookseller." "I was never teaching anywhere. I was always a bookseller," he said. "I once said to a class at Amherst that any boy who bought $100 worth of books would get the mark of A."

"I'm a book person," he often said. "All thinking and all stories go on in books." He couldn't teach in a town without a good bookstore. He called himself a "reckless reader." He told the boys that it was better to read not a thousand books, but one book a thousand times. "That's why I remember so well."

He loved to tell them the story of a snobbish old New England lady. "There were some neighbors she didn't approve of and she exclaimed, 'What would you expect? They were brought up in a bookless home.' "

That fall 1923, while the Frosts were living at 10 Dana Street in Amherst, the first family wedding took place. Carol and Lillian LaBatt had been engaged since the Long Trail hike. When Lillian had finished high school she had wanted to attend college and had enrolled at the University of Vermont. But she was partially deaf and had great difficulty in understanding her instructors there. She became discouraged and homesick and decided to drop out.

"Carol went right to her mother and got her. It was all done in a week," Frost wrote to Lincoln MacVeagh. They were married in a small wedding at the Congregational Church in East Arlington, and went to live in the Stone Cottage. Clear title to the house was Rob and Elinor's wedding gift to them.

Rob was pleased with the marriage. He found himself reliving his own early love. And Lillian was, from then on, a loving and loved member of the family, a steadying influence on her husband, and, ultimately, a source of comfort and support to her father-in-law.

Carol and Lillian had the Stone Cottage to themselves for the winter while Rob and Elinor remained at Amherst. Later the parents would move to another farm in South Shaftsbury, the Gully.

That winter of 1924 saw the temporary settling down also of two of Rob's girls. Lesley and Marjorie opened a little bookshop in Pittsfield, Massachusetts, called The Open Book, and their father was eager to help them. In June of that year, at commencement exercises at Columbia University, Rob accepted the Pulitzer Prize for *New Hampshire,* then went on a few days later to accept honorary doctorates in letters from Yale University and Middlebury College.

Rob spent the next few years swinging, like a pendulum, between Amherst and Michigan, unable to commit himself permanently to either school. The family was plagued with sickness and "scatteration" of the children.

Rob wrote to his friend Louis Untermeyer in February 1926:

> We have been East, two whole months with a sick Marjorie, and are now divided over her, Elinor having stayed on to take care of her, and I having come to Ann Arbor to make some show of teaching a little for my year's pay. . . . All this sickness and scatteration of the family."

Marjorie had pneumonia and an infection resulting from chronic appendicitis. Michigan became for them then "too far from the chil-

dren for the stretch of our heartstrings.'' Rob's concern for and devotion to his children—and to Elinor—were constant. While poetry
was, of necessity, the greatest force in his life, it would have been
nothing without his family.

"Devotion," a four-line verse that appeared in *West-Running
Brook,* his next volume of poems (published in 1928), expresses this
simply and beautifully:

> *The heart can think of no devotion*
> *Greater than being shore to the ocean—*
> *Holding the curve of one position,*
> *Counting an endless repetition.*

Rob had, and gave, the devotion that holds the curve. Marriage
to him was a lasting bond.

When Marjorie had recuperated enough to travel, Elinor took her
and Irma back to Michigan to be with Rob. It was there, in the house
on Pontiac Street, that Irma met an architect named John Paine Cone
who was visiting from Kansas. Before John left to return to Kansas
and Irma returned to Vermont, the two planned to marry.

Then suddenly in July of 1926, when the whole family was together in Vermont, Carol's wife Lillian became ill and underwent
major surgery. The situation proved too much for Rob. When Lillian
seemed sufficiently recuperated, Elinor left Irma to look after both
Lillian and Marjorie (and Carol and their two-year-old son Prescott)
and took Rob to Franconia for a much-needed rest.

It was here, in an upstairs bedroom facing Mount Lafayette, that
Rob wrote most of "West-Running Brook," the title poem of his
next book. The poem recalls the Derry days when Rob and Elinor
walked beside a stream that, strangely, flowed westward instead of
east to the Atlantic Ocean, its eventual destination.

When the wife in the poem tells her New England farmer husband
that the brook can trust itself to go by contraries, "the way I can with
you, and you with me," we know that Rob was using metaphor once
again to reaffirm his belief in marriage. He was writing another love
poem to Elinor. When it was published in 1928, the book, a study in
"contraries," was dedicated again to E. M. F.

In the spring of 1926, weary of commuting between Michigan and
New England—of running the water out of the pipes in the house on

Pontiac Street and leaving it to freeze every few weeks so he could return to Pittsfield, Massachusetts, to be with Elinor and the still-ailing
Marjorie—Rob made the decision to return to Amherst permanently.
The appointment he accepted was as full professor of English. He
would be required to spend only one term on the campus. (The Amherst school year was divided into three terms.) He would lecture and
meet students in conference—informally—for ten weeks of the year.

Rob would now have time to write poetry and to "bard around."
He would be able to protect his health (and perhaps avoid some of
his almost constant bouts with the flu) by spending the cold winter
months in Florida. He would have time to read, to lecture, even to
teach at other schools across the country, if he wished.

And this he did for the next twelve years. But those twelve years
were to bring challenges and difficulties almost too great to bear.

The first of these concerned his sister Jeanie. Her tragedy came
to an end with her death in a mental institution on September 7, 1929.
She was only fifty-three years old. Jeanie, who as a youngster could
stand on a stool in her mother's kitchen and recite the poetry of Robert
Burns; who could teach in her mother's school in Lawrence; and who,
at the age of forty, with her brother's urging and encouragement,
could put herself through the University of Michigan and earn a degree
in two-and-a-half years—finally could not cope with the world around
her. In 1920 Rob had been forced to place her in the state hospital in
Augusta, Maine, where she remained until she died.

Rob, talking to his close friend John Bartlett about Jeanie several
years later, could look back on her life and wonder if she could have
saved herself by making different choices along the way. It seemed a
miracle to him that he had made the right choices for himself.

And always, there lurked the ever-present threat of Marjorie's
illnesses. At the beginning of 1928, when Marjorie had just turned
twenty-three, she was hospitalized at Johns Hopkins University Hospital for ten weeks. Then that summer Rob and Elinor decided to take
her to Europe. They hoped that a trip abroad, combined with Marjorie's desire to see Paris and to learn to speak French, would give her
renewed energy and zest for life.

The only person Rob notified of their planned trip was his old
friend in England, the barrister-poet-botanist-book collector John W.
Haines. The Haineses promptly invited the Frosts to stay with them.

Rob and Elinor took Marjorie abroad in 1928. This is a drawing made from their passport photo. *Photo by Lawrence H. Bober, courtesy Jones Library, Amherst.*

They sailed from Quebec to Le Havre, France, then went immediately to Paris. Although Rob did not like Paris, he did try, for Marjorie's sake, to enjoy some of the sights. They went on to Sèvres, a city well known for its beautiful porcelain, and toured the ceramics museum. They spent an exciting day wandering about Versailles with its famed Hall of Mirrors in the palace, its beautiful gardens and parks.

Marjorie, however, could not seem to come out of her depression—nor to regain her physical strength. Elinor's disappointment was almost more than she could bear.

Rob decided that Elinor was more in need of diversion than Marjorie at the moment. He found a companion-nurse for Marjorie, left her in that woman's care, and took Elinor off to London. There they stayed at the old Imperial House on Russell Square for a few days until Elinor had regained her strength.

As soon as she felt strong enough, they continued on to Gloucester, where they spent ten days "hiding" with the Haines family. While Elinor rested and visited with Mrs. Haines, Rob and John walked again in the hills of Dymock. Together they botanized, and reminisced about the happy times they had spent in the area with Edward Thomas, Lascelles Abercrombie, and Wilfred Gibson. They visited the Gallows, and were saddened to see it abandoned and falling into ruin. They visited the Old Nailshop and Little Iddens. They climbed May Hill and thought all the while of how much they missed Edward Thomas.

But soon word came that Marjorie was not well in Paris, and Elinor went to get her. They took a few days to show Marjorie some of the London scenes she remembered from her childhood—then sailed for home aboard the SS *Olympic* on November 15, 1928. Heavy rains and rough seas made the voyage unpleasant for the three of them. They wondered whether the trip had been at all worthwhile for Marjorie.

Rob worried again that he had done the wrong thing for his family—that he had made Elinor unhappy by keeping her abroad longer than she had felt it wise to stay—that he had tired her and that Marjorie was none the better for it.

When they finally landed in New York, Rob was not even allowed the luxury of returning home with his wife and daughter. He had reading engagements scheduled in Baltimore, Maryland, and in Greensboro, North Carolina. It was December before he finally rejoined his family in South Shaftsbury.

While the three Frosts had been in Europe, Lesley had met and married a man named James Dwight Francis. They were waiting for Rob in South Shaftsbury also. (Unhappily, Lesley decided after a few years that she had made a mistake. In spite of her father's strong objections, she divorced James after the birth of their second daughter.)

When the entire family was gathered together again in the Stone Cottage, Rob and Elinor began to think that Carol, Lillian, and Prescott should have the house for themselves. They had never before thought there was anything unusual in continuing to live in a house that they had given as a gift. Now they realized that their children should have some privacy. Also, Rob found the hubbub was becoming too much for his nerves. He wanted a place of his own—a chance for some quiet and a time to be alone with Elinor. So he embarked once again on one of his favorite pastimes—looking for a farm to buy.

He found a 150-acre farm tucked away in a gully between two ridges of land. The cozy little eighteenth-century house had a view up the valley to the peaks of the Green Mountains, westward into New York State. There was even a stand of paper birches on the edge of one field. It was only a mile and a half from Carol's farm, or just three-quarters of a mile if he cut across the fields. In January Rob wrote to Louis Untermeyer—"I bought a farm for myself for Christmas." The five thousand dollars that it cost was readily available from Henry Holt and Company as royalty earnings from *West-Running Brook*.

It was almost a year before the renovations on the house and the farm were completed and the Frosts could move in. But they loved it immediately—particularly "the breathless quiet," as Rob wrote. They considered many names for the house—among them Marjorie's choice of "Nine Barns," in memory of the barns it once had. But it was five-year-old Prescott's choice that won out—"the Gully."

Now that they were settled Marjorie decided she wanted to study nursing at Johns Hopkins. She had been impressed by the Nurses' School when she was hospitalized there the year before. But she was destined not to complete her course. In the fall of 1930, after having done extremely well at school for almost two years, she collapsed once again. This time her illness was diagnosed as tuberculosis. Rob and Elinor were devastated. They rushed to her bedside in Baltimore. There they made arrangements for her to go to Boulder, Colorado. She would stay at the Mesa Verde Sanitorium, just three blocks from where their friends John and Margaret Bartlett were living.

Rob completed his obligations at Amherst, then threw himself into a round of readings and lectures in order to earn money to cover Marjorie's expenses in Colorado. Then just as Marjorie began to improve, another crushing blow fell. Lillian was found to have tuberculosis also. The dreaded disease seemed to be stalking them. Lillian and Carol decided then to move to California, where good treatment and a better climate were available for Lillian.

Rob was particularly distressed that these three who were so dear to him would be so far away—that he would no longer be able to watch over them—to help Carol on the farm, and to share in his grandson's growing up. "Prescott had become very precious to us. . . ." As soon as they could, Rob and Elinor made the long journey west. They went first to Colorado, to visit Marjorie. Elinor wrote from there to a friend back east:

> Marjorie doesn't seem as well as I had hoped to find her: . . . But she seems happy, and I know she will recover. . . . With Lillian it is different. I am afraid she may not live, and the great concern I feel for her, and for Carol and Prescott, stretches my endurance almost to the breaking point.

Elinor and Rob did go on—from Colorado to California to help Carol search for a house for his family. Then they found a good TB specialist and a good sanitorium for Lillian. They promised Carol they would bear the expense of medical care and hospitalization for Lillian.

Finally, satisfied that they had done all they possibly could, they headed home—but decided to go by way of San Francisco. It would be Rob's first trip back to the city in which he had been born.

Elinor was as excited as Rob at the prospect of seeing her husband's birthplace, but when they arrived in San Francisco, she was not strong enough to accompany him. While she rested in a hotel room, Rob wandered about the city alone. He walked once again on the beach below the old Cliff House and—several months later, back in Vermont—produced for his grandchildren "A Record Stride":

. . . .
I have a pair of shoes standing,
Old rivals of sagging leather,
Who once kept surpassing each other,
But now live even together.
. . . .
I wet one last year at Montauk
For a hat I had to save.
The other I wet at the Cliff House
In an extra-vagant wave.

Two entirely different grandchildren
Got me into my double adventure.
But when they grow up and can read this
I hope they won't take it for censure.

I touch my tongue to the shoes now,
And unless my sense is at fault,
On one I can taste Atlantic,
On the other Pacific salt.
. . . .

By March of 1932 Rob and Elinor, pleased at the progress that Marjorie was making at the sanitorium, were even more delighted with the news from her that she had fallen in love with a young man at the University of Colorado.

"He is a dear, kind, and considerate man, another real Victorian, Papa, with the beautiful ideals that I had feared no longer existed."

After completing obligations to read and to receive honorary degrees from Columbia University and Williams College that spring, Rob went to Colorado to meet Willard Fraser.

Marjorie's return to health and her happiness with this quiet and straightforward young archaeologist, whom her parents liked immediately, caused so much joy that the aftermath was all the more terrible. Marjorie married Willard in his home in Billings, Montana, on June 3, 1933. "The Master Speed," an unusual lyric ode in honor of a bride and groom, was Rob's gift to them:

> *No speed of wind or water rushing by*
> *But you have speed far greater. You can climb*
> *Back up a stream of radiance to the sky,*
> *And back through history up the stream of time.*
> *And you were given this swiftness, not for haste*
> *Nor chiefly that you may go where you will,*
> *But in the rush of everything to waste,*
> *That you may have the power of standing still—*
> *Off any still or moving thing you say.*
> *Two such as you with such a master speed*
> *Cannot be parted nor be swept away*
> *From one another once you are agreed*
> *That life is only life forevermore*
> *Together wing to wing and oar to oar.*

But he couldn't know then how rapidly "the rush of everything to waste" would overtake them.

In March of 1934 Marjorie gave birth to a little baby girl whom they named Marjorie Robin Fraser. Elinor was with her daughter when the baby was born and stayed for eleven days after that. Then seeing that Marjorie and the baby were fine and learning that Rob, in Amherst by himself, was ill again (he had been suffering intermittently from exhaustion, bad colds with fever, and a persistent cough), she left to return home to care for Rob.

Physical and nervous exhaustion continued to be the price Rob paid for all his speaking engagements. But he needed the money now for his children's hospital bills.

No sooner had Elinor arrived home, though, than Willard telephoned from Billings to say that Marjorie was seriously ill with puerperal fever, which sometimes affects new mothers. Rob and Elinor left for Montana immediately.

There they found that a hundred young people in Billings had offered blood for transfusions. But nothing seemed to help. Marjorie hovered between life and death. Today antibiotics are routinely used to cure this disease, but in 1934 they were not available. Then Rob, learning that a new serum was being experimented with at the Mayo Clinic in Rochester, Minnesota, arranged to have Marjorie flown the thousand miles there by private plane. A nurse and a doctor accompanied her. Willard and the Frosts drove there in Willard's car. But by the end of April there was still no sign of improvement. Her temperature was 110°, the highest ever known at the Mayo Clinic. Letters and telegrams to friends back East tell the story. Elinor wrote to the Whichers:

> The days and weeks have passed by and we are hardly aware of it, so much does this suffering and fear hold us apart from the world. . . . There is a faint hope that her resistance, which has proved so marvelous up to now, will pull her through

and Rob wrote to Louis Untermeyer:

> We are going through the valley of the shadow with Marjorie. . . . That [the serum] and blood transfusions every other day and Marjorie's tenacity and Elinor's devotion and the mercy of God are our hopes.

Then on May 2, 1934, the last telegram to the Whichers from Rob:

> Elinor's love didn't save her from loss . . .

Marjorie had succumbed. She was buried in Billings, Montana. It was two weeks before Rob could bring himself to write of it to his friend Louis Untermeyer:

Well, the blow has fallen. The noblest of us all is dead, and has taken our hearts out of the world with her. It was a terrible seven weeks' fight—too indelibly terrible on the imagination. No death in war could more than match it for suffering and heroic endurance. . . .

We were torn a fresh every day between the temptation of letting her go untortured or cruelly trying to save her. The only consolation we have is the memory of her greatness through all. . . .

We thought to move heaven and earth—heaven with prayers and earth with money. We moved nothing. . . .

Elinor took Willard and her little grandchild Robin home to Vermont for a short time. When Willard returned to Montana, Lillian, remarkably recovered from her bout with tuberculosis and home again, offered to care for Robin. She kept her at the Stone Cottage for the summer, then Elinor and Robert returned her to her father and grandmother in Billings.

Lillian and Carol continued to have Robin stay with them for several months each year in order for her to grow up in a regular family environment. Eventually, the tearing of emotions every time she was shifted from the East to the West—from one family to the other—became too much for all to bear. They decided it would be best for Robin to be brought up in Montana with her father and grandmother.

When Elinor and Rob went to Amherst after returning Robin to Montana that first fall it was obvious that Elinor had gone beyond her physical and emotional endurance. In November she suffered a heart attack. She recuperated slowly—but never fully. Elinor never accepted or forgot the loss, the suffering, the anguish of Marjorie's illness and death. To an onlooker she often appeared quiet, distant, and cool—but her eyes were always tearful.

As soon as Elinor was strong enough to travel, the doctor recommended that she spend the winter in Florida. He felt that both Elinor and Rob needed the warmth there in order to survive. Lillian's doctor had given her similar advice. So plans were made for all of them to go to Key West. By the end of December, Rob and Elinor were established in one house, with Carol and his family in another just down the road. And Prescott could spend every afternoon with his grandpa. Rob was trying hard to keep his mind off his fears and to keep his grief under the surface, where he believed the great griefs belonged.

Just a little more than a year after Marjorie died the Frosts found their heartstrings pulled once again. At Elinor's urging Rob accepted an invitation to serve on the staff of the Rocky Mountain Writers' Conference in Boulder, Colorado. Elinor had begged him to accept. She wanted to use this trip as a means of seeing little Robin again, and of visiting Marjorie's grave. The trip from Boulder to Billings was relatively short.

Although Rob feared Elinor was not strong enough to make the journey, nor to face the emotional strain it was bound to cause, he was not able to dissuade her from going. In an attempt to help her build up the needed strength, he kept the house quiet for her, discouraged visitors, and was never away from her long at a time.

Late in July they made the long, melancholy journey by train from South Shaftsbury to Boulder. Willard and his mother brought little Robin to them from Billings. Elinor's joy at holding Marjorie's "bright, forward, exceptionally merry" baby in her arms was compensation enough for the physical and emotional toll it had taken. Elinor cared for Robin during the next week, while Rob attended to his duties at the conference.

November

We saw leaves go to glory,
Then almost migratory
Go part way down the lane,
And then to end the story
Get beaten down and pasted
In one wild day of rain.
We heard " 'Tis over" roaring.
A year of leaves was wasted.
Oh, we make a boast of storing,
Of saving and of keeping,
But only by ignoring
The waste of moments sleeping,
The waste of pleasure weeping,
By denying and ignoring
The waste of nations warring.

·16·

We heard " 'Tis over" roaring

At the end of 1935, when the Frosts were once again spending the winter in Florida, Rob received an invitation that was to him perhaps the greatest honor he would receive. He was invited to be the Charles Eliot Norton Professor of Poetry at Harvard for the spring term 1936. This involved delivering a series of six lectures at Harvard, then presenting these in a manuscript for publication to the Harvard University Press.

To Rob, who as a young man had fled the Harvard halls of learning instead of completing a proper academic course, the honor was great. It proved again and finally that his choice had been a wise one. He had taken the right road. He had recognized his own pattern and had stayed with it. Robert Frost had become a brilliant and respected poet and teacher even though he had defied the conventional mode of arriving there.

At the first lecture, delivered on March 4, 1936, the audience filled every seat in the New Lecture Hall. The hall held a thousand people, but well before starting time every seat was taken and people were crowding into the aisles and even along the edge of the platform. When Rob was escorted in at eight o'clock the wild applause seemed to frighten him. Neither he nor the committee that had planned it had expected such a turnout. No one, least of all the poet himself, realized the extent of his appeal to the public.

Rob began to speak hesitantly, but the obvious warmth of his audience soon relaxed him. He used no notes, but knew exactly what he was going to say. He did not deliver a formal lecture. In fact, he appeared to wander here and there as an illustration suddenly occurred to him. But all the time he was proceeding smoothly, inevitably, and intentionally toward a point he wished to make. All over the hall people were taking notes as Rob, without any seeming effort, was giving them thoughts and phrases to turn over in their minds and to take home with them. He held his audience spellbound—at times he had them choked with emotion, then in an instant, he would turn it off with a laugh. He read from his own poems to illustrate the points he wanted to make. It was apparent to the people who heard him that they were hearing one of the greatest minds of a generation seeking for truth, and moving to its target as swiftly and surely as an arrow.

The turnout for the second lecture was even larger. People began arriving at four in the afternoon. By 7:30 there were no seats left. People sat on the floor all the way up and down the aisles. They sat on the platform steps and along the edge and on window ledges. They climbed the fire escapes and perched on the grating to hear him through the windows. Even after Rob began to speak the people continued to stream in. They were the students and faculty of all the public and private institutions in and around Boston. They were the well-known writers of the area. President and Mrs. Conant of Harvard were there. Every element of Boston society was represented. When he finished, the ovation for this great yet simple figure of a man was tremendous.

But Elinor was not there to hear him. Her custom of not attending his lectures continued even here. But she was always waiting anxiously at home to hear how his talk had come out. In this way Elinor could remain the protector of private places that were the taproot of their lives. Rob never commented. He simply said, "It was thought best. . . ."

And Rob remained true to his own pattern after the lectures. He was still a nonconformist. He never turned in to Harvard the text of his talks. Other than the notes taken by some of his listeners, and the newspaper accounts, no records remain.

Some of the poems he had read at the lectures, though, found their way into his next book. *A Further Range,* published in 1936, was dedicated once again to Elinor:

> *for what it may mean to her that*
> *beyond the White Mountains were the Green;*
> *yes, and beyond both these were the Rockies,*

Elinor in the Old Book Room at
Rockford College, Illinois, in 1935.
Courtesy Robin Hudnut.

the Sierras, and, in thought, the Andes and
the Himalayas; range beyond range even into
the realm of politics and religion.

Rob was using metaphor to say that the lives of his children had
drawn him away from New England across all the mountain ranges
in the country, and even back to his birthplace in California. It was
this that had given a new range of themes to his poetry—even social
and political.

A Further Range was awarded the Pulitzer Prize in May 1937. In
June, Harvard honored him once again. It awarded to Robert Frost
an honorary doctorate of letters.

It was only four months after they had shared the joy of the
Harvard honor that Rob and Elinor were once again "acquainted with
the night." A cancerous growth was removed from Elinor's breast.
Rob's letter to Louis Untermeyer dated October 4, 1937, reveals the
depth of his anguish:

> I doubt if she fully realizes her peril. So be careful how
> you speak in your letters. . . . She has been the unspo-
> ken half of everything I ever wrote, and both halves of
> many a thing. . . . We shall make the most of such hope
> as there is in such cases. . . . I have had almost too much
> of her suffering in this world.

The fear that the cancer might spread was not realized, and Rob
and Elinor left for Gainesville, Florida, for the winter. There they

shared a house with Lesley and her daughters. At Elinor's insistence she and Rob lived upstairs so that Rob would not be disturbed by the footsteps of the little girls overhead. Lillian and Carol, with Prescott and Robin, settled in a house nearby. The joy of being surrounded by all her grandchildren was enough to provide Elinor with renewed strength.

It was the loving and caring for her husband, her grandchildren, and her own children, who tagged after her as much after their marriages as before, that kept Elinor beautiful and content. "Rob is as considerate of Elinor as a lover in his teens," they were described then. "And her eyes shine from their depths as they rest on him."

But their joy would be short-lived. Just two months later, as they were returning from a pleasant but tiring day of house hunting in Gainesville (Robert and Elinor had decided to purchase a permanent winter home there), Elinor suddenly collapsed. The doctor was summoned immediately. He confirmed Rob's fears that Elinor had suffered a heart attack and was too ill to be moved to a hospital.

Elinor hovered between life and death for several days. Rob was so distraught that the doctor banished him from her room. He feared Rob would upset Elinor more and hasten her death. He saw how difficult it was for Rob to control his emotions.

Rob paced the corridor outside Elinor's room as she suffered successive heart attacks. He waited for the doctor to allow him to enter the room. He wanted to see her once more—to hold her hand—to have from her some word or look of assurance that their marriage had been worth its cost to her. He wanted her to tell him that the pain and the suffering of their life together, the illness, the poverty, the loss of children, had been offset by the joys and triumphs they had shared. He wanted to tell her what she meant to him. She never gave him the chance.

A brief telegram to Louis Untermeyer on March 20, 1938, told it all: "Elinor died today of a heart attack." An extraordinary relationship had come to an end.

Rob blamed himself unmercifully. Had he asked too much of her? Had he been selfish? Was her death his fault? In a terrible state of guilt and doubt, he collapsed with flu. The doctor feared it might turn into pneumonia.

His children offered little support. Lesley was overcome by grief herself and blamed him for her mother's death. Irma remained in New

Hampshire. Carol, who had leaned so completely on his mother, collapsed when she died. He returned, with Lillian, Prescott, and Robin, to the comfort of the Stone Cottage in South Shaftsbury.

After a memorial service for Elinor on April 22 in the Johnson Chapel at Amherst, Rob returned to Vermont also. But he found that he couldn't sleep in the ghost-filled farmhouse at the Gully, so Lillian and Carol made him feel welcome at the Stone Cottage. He tried to talk of ordinary things with Carol, Lillian, and Prescott. He tried to think of a way to reorganize his life. But for the most part he wandered aimlessly around the farm by himself. One day he found one showy orchis growing wild where he and Carol had planted a grove of red pine trees seventeen years before. But when he brought it home there was no one to recognize it as

> *The measure of the little while*
> *That I've been long away.*

He felt compelled to break all ties with the immediate past that he and Elinor had shared at Amherst. He resigned his professorship and sold the Sunset Avenue house. The pivot of his personal life was gone. He faced a desolate and solitary summer.

He wrote to Louis Untermeyer:

> I am so quickened by what has happened that I can't touch my mind with a memory of any kind. I can't touch my skin anywhere with my finger but it hurts like a sad inspiration. In such like condition I spent all of yesterday packing deadly personal things in the desolated house on Sunset Avenue. My strength went out of me to the last drop and then Carol carried me back to the house in South Shaftsbury. I feel as a tree that has lost its whole surrounding forest by bad forestry. . . . Carol stood by me all day like a good boy. He has got himself together. He didn't know what to do those first days.

Rob continued to brood. Had he dragged Elinor through too much of a life for one as frail as she? He wrote to J. J. Lankes, artist and friend, "I refused to be bowed down as much as she was by other deaths. But she has given me a death now that I can't refuse to be bowed down by."

> *Rain was the tears adopted by my eyes*
> *That have none left to stay.*

Toward the end of the summer Kathleen Johnston Morrison accepted Rob's plea that she become his managing secretary. Their friendship had begun many years before when Kay Johnston was a student in a seminar that Rob conducted at Bryn Mawr. Then, when Rob delivered the six Norton Lectures at Harvard in 1936, Kay, now married to Theodore Morrison, professor of English at Harvard, entertained for the Frosts at the conclusion of five of the lectures. Elinor gave the party for the last of the series. Then Rob and the Morrisons had come together once again at the Amherst service for Elinor.

Now Kay, who had recently lost her father and needed something to help her through her loss, took Rob in tow. By the fall he was able to write the poem "November." It was reminiscent of another poem of farewell he had written forty-three years before when he had feared that Elinor would never marry him. "Reluctance," the early poem, accepted the "end of a love or a season."

In "November" he accepted his loss: "We heard ' 'Tis over' roaring." He knew that he must go on. Once again, he had chosen life.

By the end of January 1939, Kay Morrison had helped Rob to make some order out of his business papers, neglected since Elinor's death. Perhaps even more important, she had helped him to find and to move into a pleasant apartment at 88 Mount Vernon Street in Boston. This was the first time he had ever lived alone.

Then on February 16, his *Collected Poems of 1939* was published. The book contained the extraordinary preface "The Figure a Poem Makes." It is probably the first writing Rob did on Beacon Hill, and was the only time he ever agreed to write anything to order. He wrote the piece at the request of William M. Sloane III, Rob's editor at Holt and the new head of Holt's trade department. The telegram Rob received from Holt the day the book was published was written partly in Latin. It was Sloane's tribute to a beloved poet and "Latinist." It stirred Rob deeply:

No satisfaction could be keener than that with which we published today your *Collected Poems. Exegisti monumentum perennius aere.* [You have reared a monument more lasting than bronze.]

The preface reflects Frost's interest in the relationship of the sounds of a poem to the sense, or meaning, the sound conveys. It states that a poem "begins in delight and ends in wisdom." It is a "momentary stay against confusion." Perhaps the writing of the preface was a momentary stay against confusion for Robert Frost.

In a letter written to his old friend Sidney Cox shortly after publication of the book, Rob wrote, "But I am very wild at heart sometimes. Not at all confused. Just wild—wild. Couldn't you read it between the lines in my Preface nay and in the lines?" Perhaps he had hoped that some of the wildness of his heart would be erased by writing about it.

But the wildness did not leave him. He kept busy during the day,

"I don't write poetry by the day or week, but by the years." The poet in 1938. *Courtesy Jones Library, Amherst.*

but he threw money away, literally throwing the change in his pockets into schoolyards and into the Charles River. He sold his only remaining copy of *Twilight,* the little book of poems he had written for Elinor so many years ago—that other time when his heart had shown a wildness at the fear of losing her. (Ten years later the collector would offer the book back to Frost for ten thousand dollars.) His only comfort at times was his newest friend, a black-and-white Border collie of Scottish descent whom he bought to ease the ache of loneliness. He named the dog Gillie. An unusual relationship developed between them. Gillie seemed instinctively to have taken his master under his watchful eye and quickly became both protector and companion.

Rob never raised his voice to the dog. When walking with a friend, Rob would make his orders to the dog part of his general conversation. "Poetry is—Gillie you may run," softly spoken, was enough and the dog would instantly take off. Yet he returned as quickly and silently if his name were mentioned in conversation again. Gillie seemed to understand, too, that his master did not enjoy an outward show of affection. When Rob came in the door after an absence of several hours Gillie would not jump, bark, or lick. He knew better than to show his love.

In May, Rob accepted the offer of a post newly created for him at Harvard, the Ralph Waldo Emerson Fellowship in Poetry. He would live at Adams House, with upperclassmen, and would teach only one seminar a week, and for one semester per year only. Once again he had the freedom he had been granted at Amherst. And once again the students loved him. They crowded into Adams House and sat spellbound through his lectures. Many were young men who would soon be going off to war (the United States was becoming more and more involved in World War II), but then they read poetry and they talked on many subjects—even their poet-professor's morning mail. They loved it when Rob told them that an artist should be able to get through college "with one brain tied behind him" and when he told them that college work was too hard. Learning should come in an offhand fashion. At the end of the course his parting words to them were "don't work—worry."

Perhaps he was thinking then that he had walked away from two colleges. But he hadn't been just a rebel. He had left because he couldn't see the difference between being intellectual in college and being in-

Rob walks the campus at Dartmouth with Gillie, his black-and-white Border collie, who helped to ease the ache of loneliness after Elinor's death. *Courtesy Dartmouth College Library*.

tellectual outside of college. He had known then that he had to find out for himself whether he had it in him to write and to think.

But his own lack of a formal college education would never allow him to respect a youngster who left school and allowed his parents to support him. He remembered well that he had worked to help support his mother and his sister from the time he was twelve years old. He wanted his own children—and his grandchildren—to have the courage to grab hold of something and work at it. He would have liked each of his children to be a specialist in one of the fields he was interested in—astronomy, architecture, math, botany.

One Step Backward Taken

Not only sands and gravels
Were once more on their travels,
But gulping muddy gallons
Great boulders off their balance
Bumped heads together dully
And started down the gully.
Whole capes caked off in slices.
I felt my standpoint shaken
In the universal crisis.
But with one step backward taken
I saved myself from going.
A world torn loose went by me.
Then the rain stopped and the blowing,
And the sun came out to dry me.

·17·

And the sun came out to dry me...

Just as Rob began his second year of teaching at Harvard he experienced another great grief.

His son Carol shot himself. Lillian had undergone serious surgery, and Carol feared she was going to die. He forgot that her spirit and strength had brought her through other illnesses. He became despondent.

Carol had had problems since childhood. He wrote poetry, some of which his father had called powerful and splendid. Rob tried to instill the self-confidence that Carol lacked. "We both liked the apple-crating poem for the genuine satisfaction it takes in the life you are living. It has a great deal more of the feeling of real work and country business than anything of mine could ever pretend or hope to have," Rob wrote to him in 1935. But nothing had been accepted for publication. He failed in farming also, although he tried desperately to make his garden as perfect as his father made his poems. He had been dependent on his mother and she was gone. He adored his wife and now she, too, appeared lost to him.

Carol phoned Rob after visiting Lillian in the hospital, and Rob, alarmed by the sound of his voice, went immediately to South Shaftsbury. They spent an entire night talking, the father trying to make the son see that he was not a failure, that he should not expect so much of himself, that he was splendid with animals and little children. But when Carol took his father to the train the next day, he remarked to him, "You always have the last word."

Several days later, sixteen-year-old Prescott tried what his grandfather had tried. He spent an entire night talking to his father. But he was no more successful. When, near dawn, Prescott could stay awake no longer, Carol went downstairs, burned all his old letters and poems, and shot himself with the deer-hunting rifle he had given Lillian as a wedding gift seventeen years before.

Prescott, awakened by the sound of the gun, knew immediately what had happened and he knew what to do. He called the police. He called his grandfather. Then he called his friends the Hollidays, but waited to go to their home with them until the police arrived.

Rob said the boy must have gotten his courage from his mother. Perhaps Rob got his courage from his mother too.

To Louis Untermeyer Rob wrote:

> I took the wrong way with him. I tried many ways and
> every single one of them was wrong. Something in me
> is still asking for the chance to try once more.

But Carol had been past reason, beyond help.

It was a year before Rob began to emerge from the darkness of this last despair. He had lost his daughter, his wife, his son in the space of only six years. But he was winning his battle to keep his sorrow beneath the surface. He could make his poetry the medium through which he could view his grief. And he could write:

> *A world torn loose went by me.*
> *Then the rain stopped and the blowing,*
> *And the sun came out to dry me.*

Rob began to realize that he could not live in a small apartment even though he was living alone. He needed space to move around in, stairs to climb, trees outside his window, quiet streets for late night walks with Gillie. Kay Morrison found a three-story Victorian house for him at 35 Brewster Street in Cambridge, and in 1941 he bought it. It became his permanent "headquarters."

Summers presented another problem. Kay and Ted Morrison had rented the Homer Noble Farm in Ripton, Vermont, from its widowed owner during the summer of 1939. The farm was conveniently close to Middlebury College, where Ted was director of the Bread Loaf Summer Writers' Conference. When toward the end of the summer Mrs. Noble decided to sell the farm, Rob suggested he buy it. He would then lease the house to the Morrisons, and he would live in the little three-room log cabin behind the house. In all, there were three houses on the three hundred wooded acres.

If the Morrisons would care for the inside of the farmhouse, Rob would maintain the outside, and hire someone to farm. He would pay his share of the food costs. Kay would provide a basket lunch for him at the cabin and he could join the family at the farmhouse for dinner. His friends would be as welcome as theirs. The Morrisons accepted his offer, and Ripton became his Vermont base. It would remain so for the rest of his life.

The days in Vermont rapidly fell into a pattern. Rob resumed his old habit of sleeping late in the morning, then breakfasting by himself on watered milk and a raw egg. From ten until three in the afternoon he might write, read, or simply think. Kay would climb the hill from the farmhouse sometime during the morning, lunch basket in hand, and work with him on whatever project needed attention. She often found him slouched in his Morris chair, legs spread out in front of him, leaning on a homemade writing board across his knees. He would be writing or reading—the poetry of Wordsworth, or Shelley, or Shakespeare. There might be notebooks strewn about on the floor. He would be wearing crumpled pants and a freshly laundered white shirt, open at the neck, perhaps a blue shirt jacket the color of his eyes over it, and blue canvas Keds. His hair, once reddish-blond, was white and thick and always tousled.

At three Rob would leave the cabin and walk the hills or putter around the farm. He searched for underground springs, he discovered hidden wild flowers. When rain from the day before had left the swamp areas wetter than usual, he would take off his shoes, leave them on a log, roll up his pants, and go in. He loved to pick his way along narrow trails, over tree trunks and boulders, under dangling branches—always keeping a watchful eye out for unusual wild flowers. Outdoors—his natural place—he was always erect, alert. Indoors, he slouched.

Rob never wrote in the afternoon. "But then, about eight P.M., I recover from the dullness of the afternoon and feel fine until about three in the morning. I also like to write a couple of hours in the morning. Used to like to teach a class at eleven. But in the afternoon I garden, go on errands, anything that doesn't count too much."

Evenings Rob had dinner with the Morrisons. But Kay could not telephone him to let him know that dinner was ready. Rob, determined to maintain his privacy and to guard his free time for writing, refused to have a telephone installed in the cabin. Instead, he stretched a clothesline, with a bell attached, from the farmhouse up the hill to the cabin. When the line was pulled from below, the bell would ring. If Rob did not hear it—or did not come immediately from the cabin or from the woods, Gillie could always be counted on to bark. Usually only two barks were needed to bring his master out. It was only in the early 1950s, after Gillie had died, that Rob finally consented to have a telephone connected.

After dinner Rob would play with the Morrisons' two young children, Ann and Bobby, then take his guests—if there were any—back to the cabin. Often guests stayed till midnight and beyond. The talk ranged from poetry to science to politics to religion. But just as his verse had in it the conversational tones of natural speech, so his speech had in it the unmistakable ring of poetry.

When his guests were ready to leave, Rob, lantern in hand, would walk them down the dirt road to the highway. Then, in the silence of a country night, he would make his solitary way back up the hill again to the cabin.

Rob went forth from Ripton to teach, to lecture, to read his poetry, to receive academic honors—but he returned here always—to the leisure and solitude he needed to make poems. It was a continuing source of nourishment for him.

The illness that used to accompany his return home after a reading was no longer a problem. Perhaps, with Elinor gone, the guilt that had always accompanied him on his trips away from her and from his poetry had disappeared.

It was here in Ripton that he found the time to read again. He began now to reread carefully the Book of Job in the Bible. Its story of a man forced to suffer a prolonged period of undeserved adversity had, for Rob, strong emotional appeal. It was easy for him to identify his own experiences with those of the biblical Job. Like Job, much had been given to Rob and much had been taken away. He decided to explore the "reason" behind human suffering. Ultimately he would write what he called his "forty-third chapter of Job," "A Masque of Reason."

In between, friends and family came to visit. He derived particular joy from his grandchildren. Lesley's two girls, Elinor and Lee, came and went often. Lillian came—and Prescott—the pride of his grandfather. Prescott became a naval architect, graduated from the University of Miami, and married a young girl from Miami. Her parents, the Gordons, looked after Rob's home in Florida when he was up north, and ultimately lived next door to him on a piece of land he gave to them. Prescott seems to be the one of the Frost children and grandchildren who fulfilled Rob's wish—that each be a specialist in one of the fields Rob was interested in.

Pig-tailed Robin was her grandfather's delight. He treasured this photograph of her, taken on her seventh birthday. *Courtesy Dartmouth College Library.*

And Robin came. Rob spent many happy days with her. He didn't worry about her—he knew she was well cared for in Montana by her father and grandparents there. But he loved her and wanted to be with her. He was able to give to Robin the feeling of having known the mother who died giving birth to her. He brought his bright-eyed Marjorie to life for Robin. Rob traveled to Montana to speak at her high school graduation. He encouraged her at Smith College. He tried hard to convince her to pursue her artistic nature and objected when she spent some time working at the Frick Museum in New York. "You'll be a self-cured ham," he told her. He wanted her to create.

He didn't want her to channel her artistic talents into anything else. When she told him she wanted to do good, he said that it was more important to do well. "All right, Grandfather," she replied in the typical Frost manner, "I'll try to do good well." "She had me there," he admitted. Robin's father, Willard Fraser, and Rob maintained a close friendship for all of Rob's life.

And through it all Rob continued to write and to teach. In 1942, *A Witness Tree* was published. The book won for Rob the Pulitzer Prize, making him the only poet ever to receive the coveted award four times. (He had won his third Pulitzer eleven years earlier for *Collected Poems*.) The book seemed to herald a new way of life—a breaking out of the prison of his loneliness. "Never Again Would Birds' Song Be the Same" evoked the memory of Marjorie and showed how, as he had often said, "each poem was a surmounting of something in life." It was, in large measure, the lyric reflection of his tragic losses. It contained also "November" and "The Wind and the Rain," quoted earlier, and "The Silken Tent," a sonnet in one sentence that is, perhaps, his most beautiful and imaginative metaphor:

> *She is as in a field a silken tent*
> *At midday when a sunny summer breeze*
> *Has dried the dew and all its ropes relent,*
> *So that in guys it gently sways at ease,*
> *And its supporting central cedar pole,*
> *That is its pinnacle to heavenward*
> *And signifies the sureness of the soul,*
> *Seems to owe naught to any single cord,*
> *But strictly held by none, is loosely bound*
> *By countless silken ties of love and thought*
> *To everything on earth the compass round,*
> *And only by one's going slightly taut*
> *In the capriciousness of summer air*
> *Is of the slightest bondage made aware.*

In 1943 Rob returned to Dartmouth College as the George Ticknor Fellow in the Humanities, bringing him back to the college he had left after less than one semester fifty-one years before. This time he would remain at Dartmouth for six years, until 1949.

"The chief reason for going to school is to get the impression fixed for life that there is a book side to everything." R. F. with students at Dartmouth. *Courtesy Dartmouth College Library*.

It was at Dartmouth that Rob developed special friendships with two young men, Edward Connery Lathem and Hyde Cox. Edward Lathem was one of his "boys" in the class of 1951. He went on, ultimately, to become dean of libraries at Dartmouth and editor of *The Poetry of Robert Frost*, published in October of 1969.

Hyde Cox reminded Rob of his lost friend Edward Thomas. It was through Cox that Rob ultimately met and developed a friendship with Andrew Wyeth, his favorite American painter. They had hoped that some of Wyeth's paintings of the people and the country Frost loved could be reproduced in a new edition of *North of Boston*. This never came to pass.

Rob became friendly also with Alfred Edwards, who came to Holt after World War II and would go on to become president of the firm. Edwards bought a home near Ripton in the Green Mountains of Vermont, and the friendship grew.

Honors continued to be heaped upon him. In 1950 the United States Senate passed a unanimous resolution extending to Robert Frost the "felicitations of the Nation which he has served so well." The honor came to celebrate what was mistakenly thought to be Rob's seventy-fifth birthday. Actually, he was seventy-six.

In 1954 the mix-up about his birth date was finally cleared up.

Four years after his seventy-fifth birthday resolution, two eightieth birthday dinners were held—one by Holt at the Waldorf-Astoria Hotel in New York, and the other at the Lord Jefferey Inn in Amherst.

At the Amherst dinner, when Rob responded to the many tributes of his friends and fellow poets by "saying" some of his poems, he included the rarely read eclogue "West-Running Brook." It brought back into the room for his children and grandchildren who were there the woman for whom it had been written.

In 1957 at age eighty-three, he returned to England to visit again the country that had first recognized him as a poet. He walked the Dymock Hills where happy memories combined with the pain of tragic loss. He received honorary degrees from Cambridge University and Oxford University, then went on to the National University of Ireland to receive one there too. He particularly enjoyed the fact that he easily understood the tribute to him at Oxford—read aloud in Latin.

Rob was honored by more than forty universities both in the United States and abroad. From each, he received a different-colored gown and hood. His Yankee practicality found a use for them: he had them cut into squares and sewn into two patchwork quilts. "It's knowing what to do with things that counts," was his tart explanation.

But he saved the Amherst hood. "That's the one where I got some education in my middle years, that's the one I keep to wear."

He continued his barding around the country. He became the best-known and best-loved poet in America. Once, as he was walking offstage after a particularly successful reading, he was overheard singing to himself, "I wish my mother could see me now." He loved to talk. Often, even in his eighties, when he was asked to speak on a college campus for one hour, he would go to the college for three days—in case anyone wanted to do some extra talking.

He would travel by train so he could talk to whomever sat next to him. One time he spoke to a lady who assumed he was a farmer. He said that he'd rather be mistaken for a farmer above all things except a baseball pitcher. He never called himself a poet until he was past forty. "Poet," to him, was a praise word.

Usually, at the conclusion of a lecture, a small gathering of about twenty people was held in someone's home. By midnight the guests would go home, but Rob was just warming up. He would remain and talk to his host and hostess until three o'clock in the morning.

Then, if someone walked him back to his hotel, Rob was likely to walk him back home again, talking all the while. Then the procedure would begin again—back to his hotel. It could go on until dawn. Colleges quickly learned to send him home in a car.

He played softball until he was eighty-five years old. He only gave it up because one day during the summer of 1959 "a very hot liner" convinced him he was "not as sure as I used to be." Had he caught the liner? Oh, yes, he'd *caught* it.

In 1958 Rob was appointed consultant in poetry to the Library of Congress. Then in 1961 he became the first poet ever to speak at the inauguration of a president of the United States. In his telegram to President John F. Kennedy, accepting his invitation to take part in his inauguration, Rob said,

> If you can bear at your age the honor of being made president of the United States, I ought to be able at my age to bear the honor of taking some part in your inauguration. . . . I am glad the invitation pleases your family. It will please my family to the fourth generation and my family of friends and, were they living, it would have pleased inordinately the kind of Grover Cleveland Democrats I had for parents.

He planned to read his poem "The Gift Outright," published almost twenty years before the ceremony. He had never written a special verse for an occasion. But when he arrived in Washington two days before the inauguration, he was so caught up in the pageantry and the excitement that he decided he would write an additional poem as a dedication, to be read just before "The Gift Outright." When he completed the forty-two-line poem, he realized that he had no time left to memorize it. He would have to read it.

As he approached the lectern bundled up in his gray overcoat, the sharp winter wind rifled his white hair. It blew at the edges of his paper. As he began to read in a halting voice, the glare of the bright sun on the white snow blurred the words. He got as far as, "This seems something for us artists to celebrate," then stopped in apparent confusion. When he muttered, "I am not having a good light here at all," the microphones picked it up. The audience applauded. Vice Pres-

"The land was ours before we were the land's. . . ." R.F. reading his poem "The Gift Outright," at the inauguration of President John F. Kennedy, January, 1961. *Courtesy* Washington Post *and Jones Library, Amherst.*

ident Lyndon Johnson got up and tried to shade his manuscript with his top hat. Rob waved him aside. Then he said, "This was to have been a preface to a poem I do not have to read." He seemed to stand up straighter, he looked out at the audience, and he began to recite from memory in a voice suddenly young and strong, "The land was ours before we were the land's. . . ."

Later, he wrote out the preface in his cramped, wiry script and gave it to Jacqueline Kennedy, the new First Lady. At the bottom of the page he wrote, "Amended copy. And now let us mend our ways."

The afternoon has been called Robert Frost's finest hour. Perhaps it was his gift outright to the American people. Or perhaps his entire life was a gift outright to all who knew him, personally or through his poems.

Robert Frost's last book, *In The Clearing*, was published when he was eighty-eight years old. This might have been his final metaphor about his life. Through his poems, he had taken his readers on a trip from the clouded pasture spring of his first poem in his first book, where he would "wait to watch the water clear, I may," along a "road less traveled," into the dark, deep woods, to a lonely clearing that he cut for himself.

From the time he was a young boy, his life had been spent confronting and overcoming difficulties. While he always looked steadily at the worst, he never lost his knack for seeing beyond. It was this courage, this Yankee optimism, that gave meaning to his life, and that was written into all his poetry. He was able, always, to see below the surface to the essential beauty at the heart of things. He never lost his sense of wonder.

> *He somehow knew*
> *. . . Earth's the right place for love:*
> *I don't know where it's likely to go better.*

Perhaps one of the secrets of Robert Frost was that by the time he was seventeen, he had learned how to say no, and to say it so that people knew he meant it. He learned early to trust his own feelings, his doubts and his certainties, his own excitements. He was able to recognize and to stay with his own pattern. When two recognized poets told him how to make his poems more acceptable, he was able to say, "No." He knew, instinctively, that their way was not right for him.

He spent the first forty years of his life trying to find his own way and his own voice as a poet. Gently but firmly, he refused to trade individuality for conformity. He would not collaborate in his writing, he would not teach where it was repetition, he would not stay where he couldn't grow.

He said, when he was eighty, that man must live by "craft and courage" to keep the world from hurrying and crowding him too much. "That's the only way you can live your own life, do what you want to do." "I don't write poetry by the day or week," he went on, "but by the years."

He called this "protective laziness." Perhaps it was the freedom he demanded for himself to live his own life. A young friend once said that he had never seen Rob glance at a watch or clock. For him, apparently, deadlines did not exist. Because of this he could accumulate an enormous store of topics to read about, to think about, and to talk about. He could speak to a class or to a large audience without any apparent preparation. His entire life was his preparation.

> *Who cares what they say? It's a nice way to live,*
> *Just taking what Nature is willing to give,*
> *Not forcing her hand with harrow and plow.*

Rob judged his poems by the same standards he applied to an ax or a hoe or a spade. They must be solid, strong, honest. He wanted his poems to be "hard." He wanted them to be precious stones. "The difference between just any pebble and a precious stone is that the pebble shines only when it's wet. I want mine to go on shining wet or dry."

He felt that a poem should "begin in delight and end in wisdom."

"A poem is never a put-up job, so-to-speak. It begins as a lump in the throat, a sense of wrong, a homesickness, a lovesickness. It is never a thought to begin with. It is at its best when it is a tantalizing vagueness. It finds its thought and succeeds; or doesn't find it and comes to nothing. . . . It has an outcome that, though unforeseen, was predestined from the first image."

"No tears in the writer," he said, "no tears in the reader."

He was not a gloomy pessimist. He was a realist. Yet he wrote some of the saddest, most plaintive lines in the English language.

But "banter is what has always saved me. You might say that banter is the way I've looked at the world—a lover's quarrel—a kind of teasing." He proved this statement over and over again, for almost all of his poems can be found to contain some form of banter.

He once suggested that a sense of humor is a protection our feelings set up against our reason. He never lost his sense of humor. But he was never more serious than when he was fooling.

During his final illness he was at the Peter Bent Brigham Hospital in Boston. Dr. George Thorn was physician-in-chief there. As such, Dr. Thorn was also head of the teaching hospital of Harvard Medical School. Therefore, he would take his young interns with him on his rounds of the patients' rooms every morning as part of their training. Rob looked forward to their brief visits each day.

Very early the morning of January 28, 1963, Dr. Thorn arrived alone—in response to a medical crisis. When Rob saw the doctor standing in the doorway, alone, he immediately understood the significance of the visit. But he was able to say to the doctor, "Traveling light today, aren't you?" Humor was, to the last, his armor against reason.

Shortly after midnight that night Robert Lee Frost died in his sleep.

Robert Frost's empty Morris chair stands symbolically in its final resting place in the cabin at Ripton. *Courtesy Lawrence H. Bober.*

Important Dates

1874   Robert Lee Frost is born in San Francisco on March 26.

1885   Death of his father, William Prescott Frost, Jr., on May 5. Travels with his mother, Isabelle Moodie Frost, and sister, Jeanie (born 1876), to Lawrence, Massachusetts.

1890   Begins to write poetry. His first poem, "La Noche Triste," is published in the Lawrence High School *Bulletin*.

1892   Meets Elinor Miriam White. Graduates from high school.

1895   Marries Elinor White on December 19. They move into an apartment with his mother and sister, and teach in Belle Frost's school.

1896   First child, Elliott, born on September 25.

1897   Enters Harvard College.

1899   Leaves Harvard, March 31. A daughter, Lesley, born April 28.

1900   Elliott dies suddenly in July. The Frosts move to a farm in Derry, New Hampshire. Belle Frost dies in November.

1901   Grandfather Frost dies.

1902   A son, Carol, born on May 27.

1903   A daughter, Irma, born on June 27.

1905   A daughter, Marjorie, born on March 29.

1906   Has several poems published. Accepts teaching position at Pinkerton Academy.

1912   In August, sails for England with his family. On October 26 his first book of poems is accepted for publication by a London publisher.

1913   *A Boy's Will* is published, April 1. Frost writes many more poems, among them "Mending Wall" and "Birches." Meets Edward Thomas, who becomes his closest friend in England.

1914   *North of Boston* is published, May 15. England declares war on Germany in August.

1915   Frosts sail home from England in February. Frost learns that Henry Holt and Company has published *North of Boston*.

1916   Beginning of literary fame. Phi Beta Kappa poet at Harvard College in June. *Mountain Interval* published in November.

1922   Writes two poems, "New Hampshire" and "Stopping by Woods on a Snowy Evening," in one night in June.

1923   *New Hampshire* is published. Returns to Amherst as professor of English. His son, Carol, marries Lillian LaBatt.

1924   *New Hampshire* is awarded the Pulitzer Prize.

1925 Appointed a fellow in letters at University of Michigan.

1926 Returns to Amherst College as professor of English. Remains there until 1938.

1928 *West-Running Brook* is published in November.

1929 Jeanie Frost dies in September after nine years in a mental institution.

1930 First *Collected Poems* is published; wins the Pulitzer Prize the following year.

1933 Daughter Marjorie marries Willard Fraser on June 3.

1934 Marjorie dies on May 2 after the birth of daughter Robin.

1936 Appointed Charles Eliot Norton Professor of Poetry at Harvard for the spring term. *A Further Range* is published.

1937 *A Further Range* is awarded the Pulitzer Prize. Elinor undergoes surgery for breast cancer.

1938 Elinor dies of a heart attack on March 20.

1939 Moves to apartment in Boston. *Collected Poems of 1939* is published. Buys farm in Ripton, Vermont, for summers.

1940 Carol Frost commits suicide in October.

1941 Buys house in Cambridge, Massachusetts.

1942 *A Witness Tree* is published.

1943 *A Witness Tree* wins the Pulitzer Prize, making Frost the only poet to receive the prize four times. Returns to Dartmouth College. Remains there until 1949.

1945 *A Masque of Reason* is published.

1947 *Steeple Bush* and *A Masque of Mercy* are published.

1954 Eightieth birthday dinners in New York and Amherst.

1961 Is first poet ever to speak at inauguration of a president of the United States.

1962 *In the Clearing* is published.

1963 Dies January 29.

A Source Guide
for Quoted Material

Chapter 6: page 56 "I have known . . ." Sergeant, Elizabeth Shepley. *The Trial by Existence*, p. 48

Chapter 7: page 67 "Our hearts . . . etc." *New Hampshire's Child* (The Derry Journals of Lesley Frost)

Chapter 8: page 79 "Anything here . . ." Sergeant, Elizabeth Shepley. *The Trial by Existence*, p. 71

page 84 "When we returned . . ." Ibid., pp. 85–86

Chapter 9: page 94 "She never told me . . ." Sergeant, Elizabeth Shepley. *The Trial by Existence*, p. 98

Chapter 10: page 102 "acquiring interest" Sergeant, Elizabeth Shepley. *The Trial by Existence*, p. 117

page 104 "it is undoubtedly . . ." Ibid., p. 112

Chapter 11: page 108 "The cottage . . ." Thompson, Lawrance. *Robert Frost: The Early Years, 1874–1915*, p. 448

page 109 "I wish . . ." Ibid., p. 448

page 111 "The closest I ever came . . ." Sergeant, Elizabeth Shepley. *The Trial by Existence*, p. 136

pages 111–112 "The Golden Room" by Wilfred Gibson, quoted by Thompson, Lawrance, in *Robert Frost: The Early Years, 1874–1915*, p. 454

page 113 "The war is an ill wind . . ." Letter to Sidney Cox dated August 20, 1914. Quoted by Sergeant, Elizabeth Shepley, in *The Trial by Existence*, pp. 139–140*

Chapter 12: page 118 "When I got to . . ." Letter to Sidney Cox dated March 13, 1915. Quoted by Sergeant, Elizabeth Shepley, in *The Trial by Existence*, p. 156

page 119 "We had little . . ." Ibid., p. 159

page 122 "What we do get. . . ." Thompson, Lawrance. *Robert Frost: The Years of Triumph, 1915–1938*, p. 35

page 127 "This morning at . . ." Ibid., p. 86

Chapter 13: page 129 "sturdily built . . ." Thompson, Lawrance. *Robert Frost: The Years of Triumph, 1915–1938*, p. 97

page 130 "some are self-made . . ." Sergeant, Elizabeth Shepley. *The Trial by Existence*, p. 200

page 131 "I want you . . ." Gould, Jean. *The Aim Was Song*, p. 188

page 131 "The chief reason for going to school . . ." *The Atlantic Monthly*, June 1951, pp. 30–31

*Also on file at Dartmouth College Library

page 132 "He was the bravest . . ." Thompson, Lawrance. *Robert Frost: The Years of Triumph, 1915–1938,* p. 94

page 132 "But walking . . ." Sergeant, Elizabeth Shepley. *The Trial by Existence,* p. 213

page 133 "I really like least . . ." Letter dated November 7, 1917, Frost, Robert. *The Letters of Robert Frost to Louis Untermeyer,* pp. 62–63

page 136 "So one morning . . ." Spoken to Elizabeth Shepley Sergeant and quoted in *The Trial by Existence,* p. 234

page 136 "I wasn't taken . . ." Letter dated November 11, 1920. Ibid., p. 118

Chapter 14: page 141 "They are children . . ." Thompson, Lawrance (ed.). *Selected Letters of Robert Frost,* p. 276

page 141 "Our art . . ." Frost, Robert. *Letters of Robert Frost to Louis Untermeyer,* p. 146

page 142 "best bid . . ." spoken to Elizabeth Shepley Sergeant and quoted in *The Trial by Existence,* p. 251

page 145 "I had promised . . ." Thompson, Lawrance. *Robert Frost: The Years of Triumph, 1915–1938,* p. 214

page 146 "I have felt him . . ." Ibid., p. 227

Chapter 15: page 150 "I was never . . ." Lathem, Edward Connery (ed.). *Interviews with Robert Frost*

page 151 "We have been East. . . ." Letter dated February 11, 1926, Frost, Robert. *The Letters of Robert Frost to Louis Untermeyer,* pp. 177–178

page 156 "Marjorie doesn't seem . . ." Letter from Elinor Frost to Mrs. Fobes dated August 2, 1931; quoted by Thompson, Lawrance. *Robert Frost: The Years of Triumph, 1915–1938,* p. 394

page 157 "He is a dear . . ." Ibid., p. 400

page 159 "The days and weeks . . ." Letter from Elinor Frost dated April 22, 1934. Quoted by Sergeant, Elizabeth Shepley, in *The Trial by Existence,* p. 330

page 159 "We are going through . . ." Letter dated April 29, 1934, Frost, Robert. *Letters of Robert Frost to Louis Untermeyer,* p. 240

page 160 "Well, the blow has . . ." Letter dated May 15, 1934. Ibid., pp. 241–242

Chapter 16: page 165 "I doubt if . . ." Letter dated October 4, 1937, Frost, Robert. *Letters of Robert Frost to Louis Untermeyer,* pp. 295–296

page 167 "I am so quickened . . ." Letter dated May 16, 1938. Ibid., p. 308

page 169 "No satisfaction could . . ." Thompson, Lawrance. *Robert Frost: The Later Years: 1938–1963,* p. 38

Chapter 17: page 174 "I took the wrong way. . . ." Letter dated October 26, 1940, Frost, Robert. *Letters of Robert Frost to Louis Untermeyer,* pp. 322–323

pages 175–176 "But then, about eight P.M. . . ." *The Christian Science Monitor,* December 21, 1955

page 181 ". . . not as sure. . . ." *Life,* December 1, 1961, pp. 103–104

page 181 "If you can bear. . . ." Thompson, Lawrance. *Robert Frost: The Later Years, 1938–1963,* p. 278

page 184 "A poem is never. . . ." Letter dated January 1, 1916, Frost, Robert. *Letters of Robert Frost to Louis Untermeyer,* pp. 21, 22, 23

Bibliography

BOOKS

Anderson, Margaret Bartlett. *Robert Frost and John Bartlett: The Record of a Friendship.* New York: Holt, Rinehart and Winston, 1963.

Barry, Elaine. *Robert Frost on Writing.* New Brunswick, NJ: Rutgers University Press, 1973.

Burnshaw, Stanley. *Robert Frost Himself.* New York: George Braziller, 1986.

Cole, Donald B. *Immigrant City: Lawrence, Massachusetts, 1845–1921.* Chapel Hill: University of North Carolina Press, 1963.

The Committee on the Frost Centennial of the University of Southern Mississippi. *Robert Frost: Centennial Essays.* "A Day in the Life of Robert Lee Frost—1874," by William Gahagan; "The Critics and Robert Frost," by Reginald Cook. Jackson, MS: University Press of Mississippi.

Cox, Hyde, and Lathem, Edward Connery, eds. *Selected Prose of Robert Frost.* New York: Holt, Rinehart and Winston, 1966.

Cox, Sidney. *Robert Frost: Original Ordinary Man.* New York: Henry Holt and Company, 1929.

Cox, Sidney. *A Swinger of Birches.* New York: New York University Press, 1957.

Evans, William R. *Robert Frost and Sidney Cox: Forty Years of Friendship.* Hanover, NH: University Press of New England, 1981.

Frances, Robert. *Frost: A Time to Talk.* Amherst, MA: University of Massachusetts Press, 1972.

Frost, Lesley. *New Hampshire's Child: The Derry Journals of Lesley Frost.* Albany, NY: State University of New York Press, 1969.

Frost, Robert. *The Letters of Robert Frost to Louis Untermeyer.* New York: Holt, Rinehart and Winston, 1963.

Frost, Robert. *Selected Letters of Robert Frost.* Ed. by Lawrance Thompson. New York: Holt, Rinehart and Winston, 1964.

Gould, Jean. *The Aim Was Song.* New York: Dodd, Mead & Company, 1964.

Lathem, Edward Connery, ed. *Interviews with Robert Frost.* New York: Holt, Rinehart and Winston, 1966.

Lathem, Edward Connery, and Thompson, Lawrance. *Robert Frost and the Lawrence, Massachusetts, "High School Bulletin": The Beginning of a Literary Career.* New York: The Grolier Club, 1966.

Lewis, Oscar. *San Francisco: Mission to Metropolis*. Berkeley, CA: Howell-North Books, 1966.

Mertins, Louis. *Life and Talks Walking*. Norman, OK: University of Oklahoma Press, 1965.

Morrison, Kathleen. *Robert Frost, A Pictorial Chronicle*. New York: Holt, Rinehart and Winston, 1974.

Munson, Gorham. *Robert Frost: A Study in Sensibility and Good Sense*. Port Washington, NY: Kennikat Press, Inc., 1927 (reissued 1968).

Orton, Vrest. *Vermont Afternoons with Robert Frost*. Rutland, VT, and Tokyo: Academy Books, 1971.

Pritchard, William H. *Frost: A Literary Life Reconsidered*. New York: Oxford University Press, 1984.

Sergeant, Elizabeth Shepley. *The Trial by Existence*. New York: Holt, Rinehart and Winston, 1960.

Smythe, Daniel. *Robert Frost Speaks*. Boston: Twayne Publishers, 1964.

Thompson, Lawrance. *Robert Frost: The Early Years, 1874–1915*. New York: Holt, Rinehart and Winston, 1966.

Thompson, Lawrance. *Robert Frost: The Years of Triumph, 1915–1938*. New York: Holt, Rinehart and Winston, 1970.

Thompson, Lawrance, and Winnick, R. H. *Robert Frost: The Later Years, 1938–1963*. New York: Holt, Rinehart and Winston, 1976.

Thornton, Richard, ed. *Recognition of Robert Frost*. New York: Henry Holt and Company, 1937.

Walsh, John Evangelist. *Into My Own*. New York: Grove Press, 1988.

PERIODICALS

"Amherst Honors Robert Frost." *Amherst Alumni News,* April 1954.

Ciardi, John. "Robert Frost: Master Conversationalist at Work." *Saturday Review,* 21 March, 1959, 17–20.

Ciardi, John. "Robert Frost: The Way to a Poem." *Saturday Review,* 12 April, 1958, 13–15, 65.

Cook, R. L. "This New England: A Walk with Robert Frost." *Yankee,* November 1955, 18–27.

Frost, Lesley. "Our Family Christmas." *Redbook,* December 1963, 45.

Frost, Lesley. "Robert Frost Remembered." *The American Way,* March 1974, 12–17.

Hall, Donald. "Vanity, Fame, Love, and Robert Frost." *Commentary* 64 (1977), 51–61.

Harris, M. "Pride and Wisdom of Two Great Old Poets." *Life,* December 1961, 103–4.

Hindus, Milton. "Reminiscences of Robert Frost." *Midstream,* November 1979, 52–57.

Maxwell, Margaret. "Swinger of Birches: Robert Frost Remembered." *Scholastic Teacher,* 19 October 1967, 10–11.

McLam, James W. "My Business with a Poet." *Vermont Life* 18 (1963): 41–43.

Morrison, Theodore. "The Agitated Heart." *The Atlantic Monthly,* July 1967, 72–79.

"Pawky Poet." *Time,* 9 October 1950, 76–82.

"Poetry and School." *The Atlantic Monthly,* June 1951, 30–31.

"Robert Frost Up Country." *Yankee,* November 1955.

"Sherman Adams to Accept Robert Frost Award." *Conning Tower Gleanings* (Plymouth State College Alumni Association Journal), Spring 1970, 4.

Tatara, Walter T. "And Gladly Teach: Robert Frost as a Teacher." *Conning Tower Gleanings* (Plymouth State College Alumni Association Journal), Spring 1970, 5–7.

DOCUMENTS

Collection of correspondence between Robert Frost and Sidney Cox, Dartmouth College Library, Archives Department, Baker Memorial Library, Hanover, New Hampshire.

POETRY

Frost, Marjorie. *Franconia.* New York: The Spiral Press, 1936.

Frost, Robert. *The Poetry of Robert Frost.* Edited by Edward Connery Lathem. New York: Holt, Rinehart and Winston, 1969.

Frost, Robert. *The Road Not Taken.* Edited by Louis Untermeyer. New York: Holt, Rinehart and Winston, 1965.

Frost, Robert. *You Come Too: Favorite Poems for Young Readers.* London: The Bodley Head, 1964.

Palgrave, Francis Turner, ed. *The Golden Treasury of Songs and Lyrics.* London: Macmillan & Company, 1892.

Thomas, Edward. *Selected Poems of Edward Thomas.* Edited by R. S. Thomas. London: Faber and Faber, 1964.

Poetry Index

POEMS REFERRED TO IN TEXT

Indicates poem quoted in part or in full

Subject Index

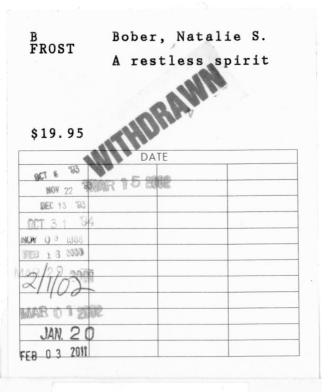